Reweaving the

Social Tapestry

THE AMERICAN ASSEMBLY was established by Dwight D. Eisenhower at Columbia University in 1950. Each year it holds at least two nonpartisan meetings that give rise to authoritative books that illuminate issues of United States policy.

An affiliate of Columbia, the Assembly is a national, educational institution incorporated in the state of New York.

The Assembly seeks to provide information, stimulate discussion, and evoke independent conclusions on matters of vital public interest.

THE AMERICAN ASSEMBLY
Columbia University

Reweaving the Social Tapestry

Toward a Public Philosophy and Policy for Families

Don S. Browning
and
Gloria G. Rodriguez

W. W. Norton & Company
New York • London

For information about permission to reproduce selections from
this book, write to Permissions, W. W. Norton & Company, Inc.,
500 Fifth Avenue, New York, NY 10110

The text of this book is composed in New Baskerville,
with the display set in New Baskerville
Composition by Carole Desnoes
Manufacturing by the Haddon Craftsmen, Inc.
Book design by Julia Druskin
Production manager: Amanda Morrison

Library of Congress Cataloging-in-Publication Data

Browning, Don S.
Reweaving the social tapestry : toward a public philosophy and policy
for families / Don S. Browning and Gloria G. Rodriguez.
p. cm. — (Uniting America)
At head of title: The American Assembly, Columbia University.
Used as background reading for the 97th American Assembly,
Kansas City, Sept. 21–24, 2000.
Includes bibliographical references and index.
ISBN 0-393-32272-6 (pbk.)
1. Family—United States—Philosophy. 2. Family policy—United
States. I. Rodriguez, Gloria G. II. American Assembly. III. Title.
IV. Series.

HQ535 .B76 2002
306.85'0973—dc21   200103408

W. W. Norton & Company, Inc., 500 Fifth Avenue
New York, N.Y. 10110
www.wwnorton.com

W. W. Norton & Company Ltd., Castle House
75/76 Wells Street, London W1T 3QT

1 2 3 4 5 6 7 8 9 0

Contents

Preface

This volume was commissioned for a national Assembly on American families, and for subsequent Assemblies and meetings throughout the United States. This program is the third in an American Assembly series on *Uniting America: Toward Common Purpose*, which was developed to offer concrete policy recommendations, based on the consensus developed from a diverse spectrum of people working together to achieve solutions to some of our country's most divisive issues.

As a core unit of society, families can play a vital role in bringing America to greater unity. Yet even the definition of "family" is a source of great division. The very meaning of the word family has changed considerably over the course of the last thirty years. It no longer always refers to the traditional image of a man and woman, married, and their children. In the twenty-first century, "family" has a multitude of definitions and, for some people, includes blended families, single-parent households, grandparents raising children, and gay and lesbian couples raising children, among others. To many, the traditional family is an ideal to be protected and encouraged. To others, the very notion of the traditional family is highly problematic, or fails to represent their reality. Moreover, economic forces, government policies, the practices of the workplace, and popular culture, while sometimes designed to help, have also negatively impacted families.

Don S. Browning, director of the Religion, Culture and Family Project at the University of Chicago Divinity School and professor of ethics and social sciences, and Gloria G. Rodriguez, founder, president, and CEO of Avance, Inc. Family Support and Education Programs, are the authors of this book, which seeks to develop a public philosophy for policies about families.

Drafts of the chapters in this volume were used as background by fifty-three leaders from American government, business, labor, law, academia, nonprofit organizations, the media, and different religious faiths and faith based organizations who gathered at the Westin Crown Center and The Conference Center at Kauffman Legacy Park in Kansas City, Missouri, for the Ninety-Seventh American Assembly, September 21–24, 2000. Dr. Browning and Dr. Rodriguez served as codirectors of this Assembly where the participants worked to define policies and offer concrete recommendations to offset the complex challenges facing American families. Among the specific issues addressed were the following:

- What are the values underlying the debates about families?
- How can we translate our diverse cultural, religious, and philosophic traditions into a common understanding of the nature and role of families?
- To what extent is pro-marriage culture important for the overall health of families?
- Where can we find the best practical help for families? What are the respective roles of government, business, labor, parents, and civil society, among others?
- What reforms need to occur in our tax system and other federal programs to help strengthen families?

Following their discussions, the participants issued a report that is included in this book and is also available on

The American Assembly's website (www.americanassembly. org or AOL keyword: American Assembly), along with information about other Assembly programs.

The *Uniting America* series commenced with an Assembly on economic growth and opportunity, and resulted in the publication of the book *Updating America's Social Contract: Economic Growth and Opportunity in the New Century*, by economists Rudolph G. Penner, Isabel V. Sawhill, and Timothy Taylor. The second Assembly in the series addressed religion and public life and was chaired by Martin E. Marty. He also wrote an introduction to the book *Religion in American Public Life: Living with Our Deepest Differences*, which contains chapters by Azizah Y. al-Hibri, Jean Bethke Elshtain, and Charles C. Haynes. The two other topics in the series are racial equality and improving intersectoral cooperation among business, government, and nonprofit world (civil society) and citizens necessary to help move our society toward common purpose in the twenty-first century.

A distinguished national Leadership Advisory Group helped to design the series and will convene in early 2002 to issue an overview report of the principal findings and recommendations from the entire series and launch a major initiative designed to catalyze a national dialogue around the key issues. The dialogue will include high-level briefings, web-based discussions, deliberations through a network of organizations from all sectors, and community meetings. This leadership group is cochaired by three American Assembly trustees, David R. Gergen, Karen Elliott House, and Donald F. McHenry, and by Paul H. O'Neill, chairman of ALCOA Inc. A list of the members of the Leadership Advisory Group is included in this book. This series will undertake not only to make the necessary recommendations, but will also develop action plans and follow-on activities necessary to achieve their policy recommendations.

The American Assembly gratefully acknowledges those funders whose generous support helped to make the Assembly on families possible:

Major funders:
The McKnight Foundation
Hallmark Corporate Foundation
The Ewing Marion Kauffman Foundation

Other significant funders:
Foundation for Child Development
Annie E. Casey Foundation

Our appreciation is also expressed to those who have funded the *Uniting America* series overall or a portion thereof:

The Ford Foundation
The Goizueta Foundation
The Lilly Endowment, Inc.
The Henry Luce Foundation, Inc.

Surdna Foundation, Inc.
The Coca-Cola Company
Robert W. Woodruff Foundation
Walter and Elise Haas Fund
Xerox Corporation
Bradley Currey, Jr.
WEM Foundation

Robert Abernethy
Genuine Parts Company
King & Spalding
Herman Russell
SunTrust Banks, Inc.
Wachovia Bank
Eleanor B. Sheldon

The policy views expressed in this volume are those of the authors and do not necessarily reflect the views of The American Assembly nor its funders or participants.

It is our hope and belief that this volume and the future Assemblies in the *Uniting America* series will help to stimulate a national dialogue that contributes to a more united America.

                                        Daniel A. Sharp
                                        President and CEO
                                        The American Assembly

Reweaving the
Social Tapestry

1

Traditions and
Public Philosophy

The authors of this short book are, from several points of view, quite different. From other perspectives, we are very much alike. Such statements, of course, can be made about any two Americans. Most Americans have at least some things in common. But vast numbers of us come from different parts of the country, are raised by different parents, belong to different religious and cultural traditions, have different kinds of education, may be of different colors, and are familiar with and possibly even speak different languages.

All of these general statements are true of the two of us, Rodriguez and Browning. The names alone suggest a great deal. Rodriguez—must be Latino. Browning—must be Anglo-Saxon. Rodriguez—might come from Mexico, Central America, South America, or Spain. Browning—bet he's from English stock. Wasn't there a poet or two by that name? Rodriguez—most likely from the Southwest or West, but increasingly could be from anywhere in the U.S. Browning—could be Midwest, North, or East, but increasingly could be from anywhere in the U.S. Rodriguez—most likely a Roman

Catholic. Browning—probably a Protestant, maybe Episco-palian. Or he might just be a stone-cold secularist.

If these are associations that pop into your mind when you read our names, you are close to the truth. Rodriguez's paternal grandparents came from Spain, and her father came from Mexico. Her maternal grandparents came from Mexico and her mother from Texas. Browning traces his family from Missouri back to Arkansas and then Virginia and, yes, finally to England. But he enjoys no direct relation to the poets. Browning is Protestant, but a liberal and low-church Protestant with little experience of the Anglican tra-dition. Rodriguez has a great deal of love and respect for the *La Virgen de Guadalupe*. Browning has only visited the virgin's shrine in Mexico City as a tourist. Browning has spent many years as an academic in a midwestern university. Rodriguez has a Ph.D. in early childhood education but has spent most of her career building Avance, one of the largest and oldest parent education and family support agencies for Hispanics in the country.

It is safe to say that we do have different backgrounds. But, as you will see, there are similarities. Our task is to take both our differences *and* similarities and think about the outlines of a consensus on a wide range of divisive issues confronting our society about families—their present condi-tion and future prospects. That's right: we are to try our hand at projecting a consensus on one of the most con-tentious subjects facing Americans—how to understand and evaluate what is happening to families and propose policies that will help them in the future.

This includes attending to the basic issue of whether we should even care, i.e., whether family disruption is a real issue. Many people believe that families, and especially mar-riage, in their customary forms are passé. Families? Oh, yawn. Boring. We can hear it now, at least in some quarters. But in case you have not noticed, our society has been for at least twenty years in a ferocious battle about the health and well-being of American families. Political and religious con-servatives used to dominate the family rhetoric, but no longer is that the case. Cultural and religious liberals also have joined the fray.

Pick up any major urban newspaper—such as the *New York Times, Chicago Tribune,* or *Dallas Morning News*—and you will read in a single issue between five to ten articles on a wide variety of family topics. Are our children out of control? Do we live in an increasingly *Fatherless America*—the title of a recent widely read book? Are mothers working too much outside the home? Is divorce damaging nearly everyone, not only children but mothers, fathers, and even the wider society? Is cohabitation a good or bad thing? Are the Republicans or the Democrats going to dominate the "family values" debate in the next election? Will advances in reproductive technology destroy families, marriage, and even the character of Americans? Is marriage going out of style? Will corporations finally catch on that it is to their advantage to support families, possibly even marriage? What do changing demographics—the increase of Hispanic and Asian populations—mean for emerging family issues?

So that's our task—to bring some order and consensus into this morass of contentious and confusing issues. From the outset, however, we must keep our goals within realistic boundaries. We cannot and will not come up with a blueprint that will settle all issues, nor will we fashion a declaration that all Americans will immediately recognize and therefore sign on the dotted line. But we will try to develop an outline, a general point of view, and a framework that might serve as a *rough* consensus. We hope to develop a point of view that will bring Americans a little closer together. We want to make sufficient progress so that our society can accomplish certain tasks in supporting families and helping them flourish.

If the two of us can come to a meeting of minds, that will be good. It also might be a sign of hope that others can make progress. But our task is to go beyond a conversation with each other. In this book, the two of us will need to exercise our imaginations. We must ask the question: with our respective understandings of the various voices in American

life and our sense of their concerns, what might be the
grounds for a working agreement on family issues? Both of
us have had a chance over the years to be in conversation
with a wide range of individuals and groups who participate
in the American debate about the family. Rodriguez, in
founding and developing Avance, has been in conversation
with parents, government officials, family researchers, universities, foundations, social workers, parent education and
child advocacy organizations, and ethnic groups beyond the
Hispanic community. Browning has directed a large research project on the family at the University of Chicago
that has brought him into conversation with economists, political scientists, feminists (both religious and secular), marriage educators, and faith communities (evangelical, liberal,
Roman Catholic, black, Jewish, Islamic). We have each written books about our experiences and research.[1]

We hope to bring these various voices and their interests
into the task of projecting a vision for a rough consensus on
our nation's concerns about its families.

A Public Philosophy for Public Policy

Although this book is about developing a consensus to
guide American public life on family issues, it is about both
public philosophy *and* public policy. We make a distinction
between the two. Public policy is often thought to refer to
the principles that guide government, legislative bodies, and
courts in developing their respective policies affecting various American groups. Public policy is concrete. It tries to establish general guidelines for specific programs and make
concrete predictions about their possible consequences. We
will advance several public policy proposals.

Public philosophy, however, is more abstract and general;
it tries to develop the framework that defines the relation
between different sectors of society as they might work together for the common good. A public philosophy, in contrast to public policy, should clarify the general principles of
justice and the specific goods that justice should actualize.

Such definitions provide the background assumptions that guide public policy. But a public philosophy is interested in more than governmental institutions and policies. It also must develop a model of how government, market, and the institutions of civil society (churches and synagogues, neighborhood organizations, PTAs, local service clubs, etc.) can work together for the betterment of the social whole. A public philosophy is about how to position the various contributions from different spheres of society. It should help clarify the special emphases and limits of these spheres and propose ways for orchestrating them for fruitful cooperation. A public philosophy for families might go so far as to clarify general obligations of parents to children and husbands and wives to one another. It might also meditate on the responsibilities of neighborhoods to families, children, and the elderly. A public philosophy should foster images of the common good and positive attitudes about their attainment.

The 1996 welfare reforms are examples of public policy. Traditional welfare such as Aid to Families with Dependent Children, it was argued, was alienating families from the world of paid work, creating dependencies, discouraging marriage, and isolating mothers and children from the wider community. Republicans and Democrats alike joined to form a unique coalition and together voted to turn welfare over to the fifty states, connect it to work, place time limits on how long a family could receive it, and to administer welfare through groups strongly identified with local communities. This was a new public policy, the merits of which our society is now trying to assess.

But this bold move had a public philosophy behind it. Our society is in the process of evaluating this as well. It contained a philosophy of more limited government, of cooperation between government and the institutions of civil society, of bringing services to the local level, of using welfare resources to enable the unemployed to gain work skills and become more self-sufficient, and of even bringing faith communities into partnership with state governments to assist the needy. This book will deal with public philosophy, but issues of public policy pertaining to specific programs will be prominent as well.

The Basic Message

Does the book have a basic message? It does. It goes like this: *a consensus on family issues in the United States can best be achieved when the family philosophies of various cultural and religious traditions are acknowledged, understood, respected, taken seriously, strengthened, brought into conversation with one another, and the positive analogies between them identified and built upon.* We also have a subordinate thesis: not only must we take cultural and religious traditions seriously on family issues, but *that the traditions themselves must learn to speak to and cooperate with other spheres and sectors of society—government, market, and various institutions of civil society.* Family issues are not just private matters that concern only particular family units and the individuals within them. Nor are family matters strictly cultural and religious issues, even though we argue that they should be viewed, at least in part, from this angle of vision. Cultural and religious traditions need to understand why governments are and should be interested in families, have been for centuries, and have every right and responsibility to be so. Cultural and religious traditions also need to understand that it is to the benefit of everyone if the market (small businesses, corporations, and other entrepreneurs) also becomes interested in families. Finally, cultural and religious traditions need to relate to other parts of civil society on family matters. These traditions should "do their own thing," that is, be themselves and affirm their own heritages, but they also should develop networks of cooperative relationships with other parts of society.

We realize that taking traditions seriously on family matters is a very specific and somewhat risky strategy. Some points of view would say that a consensus can occur only if debates and policy development go around or by-pass these traditions. Cultural traditions are often closely associated in the popular mind with religious traditions. Although there is some truth in this, it can be an oversimplification. Religion and culture are not identical. However this debate is resolved, the word *tradition* certainly refers to the past and, in the minds of many people, the past is the problem and not a source of solutions. Many people believe that it is best to keep the past out of the picture and think only about the future—in fact, make up entirely new rules to cope with what the future is bringing. Cultural and religious traditions, some believe, are backward and contentious. Ignore them if you can. Court them at your own risk. It is like swimming in a motel pool after dark with no life guard on duty.

The futurists have wisdom, but when they disconnect themselves too much from the past they lose insight, orientation, and connectedness. This is especially true with regard to the question of family. We simply cannot get oriented to what families are and what afflicts them if we don't know how family patterns emerged in the U.S. and other Western societies like it. We have to have a sense of history. To be more specific, if we do not know how Judaism and early Christianity interacted with Greco-Roman societies on family issues, how the emerging Roman Catholic Church interacted with Roman and German law to create canon law codes governing family formation and dissolution, how these codes influenced medieval Europe, how all this was both retained yet transformed by the Protestant Reformation, and how the traditions of the Reformation created the family law and customs of many Western societies, including most—although not all—states in the U.S. (Roman Catholic canon law had direct influence in several Southern and Western states), we will get confused about where we are and how to move toward the future.[2] We know we said a mouthful in this last sentence. We will return to a more detailed discussion of the historical sources of Western family traditions later in the book. But we must say this now: although it is important to know that history, we will not confine ourselves to that history. We must know our histories in order to move toward the future. We must be rooted in order to grow.

Understanding this history will explain why Rodriguez and Browning, in spite of their many differences, have enough common experience and convictions to write a book together. Furthermore, these religious, cultural, legal, and social traditions that had so much to do with shaping American lore and law about families are now interacting with other powerful traditions—Islamic, Hindu, Buddhist, neo-Confucian, Native American—that not only want social space to exercise their own family identities but eventually will want their say on issues pertaining to the larger public philosophy concerning families.

To address the future, we must know and respect the past. To think productively about the directions we should go, we must know and respect the major cultural traditions functioning in our society that represent the accomplishments—and, yes, the defects—of the past. To correct, adjust, or critique the wisdom of our various cultural traditions, we must understand and respect them. We must not ignore and disregard them. And critiquing these traditions, at certain points, is something we will do from time to time in this book. But criticism is only useful if one first understands what these traditions still can contribute to our ideas and ideals of family and marriage. The various family traditions shaping our society are not in complete contradiction with one another, but they may be in tension with each other. They also are in tension with a modernizing process that tends to ignore and disregard them. There are many points of similarity between these various traditions. We all can become preoccupied with their differences—become offended, stomp and scream over the idiosyncrasies of another tradition, and bang our heads against a wall because it will not agree with our good sense. If we are looking for differences, we can always find them; but to become preoccupied with them may blind us to huge areas of overlap, analogy, and similarity, which are the stuff of a common public philosophy.

We will not take on every issue at stake in the American family debate. We will not solve the abortion debate. Nor will we solve the matter of homosexual marriage, although we will try to clarify the issues involved in this question. These are important matters, and society should continue trying to resolve the debate over these polarizing issues. We believe, however, that these topics have so dominated our public discourse that they have drawn attention away from other extremely important issues about which Americans might more easily agree. Society should not indefinitely delay thought and action on an entire range of other important family topics until these two so-called hot-button issues are resolved.

We will do our best to address other important issues about which our society actually might develop workable agreements. Hence, this book will grapple with such topics as the well-being of children, father absence, the challenges and declining well-being of many single parents (especially single mothers), the implications of divorce and nonmarital births, the implications of the growing pattern of cohabitation, and the possible consequences of the continuing decline of marriage. These issues are all highly contentious in their own right.

A Concern for All Families

The two of us are interested in addressing the needs of all families. We will use a broad definition of families. Families are defined as some arrangement whereby one or more adults—by either biological procreation, legal action (adoption, foster parents), or other circumstances—have assumed the central responsibility for raising children. This certainly includes adults raising children in the present. But it also includes older parents and grandparents whose children have moved out of the home; they still have responsibilities to their sons, daughters, and grandchildren, and these offspring have responsibilities for them. This definition includes intact families, single-parent families, step families, traditional breadwinner fathers and domestic mothers, two-income families, blended families, ethnic families (black,

Hispanic, Asian, Muslim, American Indian, etc.), biracial families, and others (gays and lesbians raising children, grandparents responsible for children). This broad definition of family is useful for both public philosophy and public policy; see, for instance, how all these families with children would be included in certain universal entitlements that we propose in chapter 7.

But this broad definition does not mean we will ignore the question of whether some family forms are better able to discharge their responsibilities, especially to children, than others. Nor will it blind us to the question of the role of marriage in family formation. A cohabiting couple with their children are a family. A divorced single mother and children are a family and deserve respect and support from extended family, church, government, and market. Recognizing this, however, should not lead us to disregard the emerging cultural and social science discussions that are reevaluating the average consequences of divorce, nonmarital births, and cohabitation for both couples and children. We hope to face these emerging facts with an air of generosity and support. Hey! We live in a tough world for marriage and family, and we will work to show why that is true. This book may seem a bit too pro-marriage for some. Some will feel we are being judgmental and insensitive to the unmarried. Yet, we fully acknowledge that there are often good reasons for divorce and other family disruptions. Let us say this now: we do not expect our arguments and proposals to lead society to jump out of its skin so that all people become happily married for ever after. In fact, we don't even believe all people should get married; our respective traditions teach us to have great respect for the vocation of singleness. But we do hope to show how the solution to many family issues requires turning the corner a bit—and maybe quite a bit—on the role and health of marriage in our society. This, in the end, is what most people in our society want and hope for—for themselves if possible but even more for their children.

A few more words about what makes a family are still needed. A married couple who presently do not have children are not, within our definition, a family. They are a married couple—a very fine and honorable thing to be. Each member of the couple belongs to a family since they both have families of origin. But they are not as a unit a family even though they may be on the way to becoming a family. The idea of family entails adults having, or once having had, the responsibility for raising children. This is a small point, but it can make a difference for both a public philosophy and public policy of families.

We especially have in mind the emerging ethnic diversity of American families. We must be aware of the great demographic shifts presently taking place in the U.S. Americans, up until recent decades, have largely consisted of groups that came from Northern, Southern, and Eastern Europe. African Americans made up the largest minority group. All of this is changing and changing rapidly. For example, as recently as 1997, Hispanics comprised 30 million people, or 11 percent of the U.S. population. Those groups hailing mostly from the various parts of Europe, inadequately referred to as whites, made up 73 percent of the population. However, Hispanic groups are growing rapidly in comparison to both African Americans and non-Hispanic whites. The 1990 census counted 22.3 million Hispanics, a 53 percent increase since 1980. That same census counted 29.9 million blacks, only a 13 percent increase since 1980. By the year 2000, Hispanics comprised 15 percent of the U.S. population for a total of 39 million people. By 2010, Hispanics will be the largest minority group for a total of 41 million as compared to a projected 37.5 million African Americans. Today this growing Hispanic population is disproportionately poor and undereducated. Around 2030, the 73 percent "white" population of the late 1990s will have shrunk to 60.5 percent, *and by 2060, if present trends continue, blacks, Hispanics, and Asians will match or exceed the population of whites.*[3] And if we really stretch our imaginations into the future, based on present projections, Hispanics could someday become the largest group of Americans. Today we talk much about cultural diversity; tomorrow we will truly live it. This has implications for a public philosophy of families, especially the question of how we will get along in a diverse society.

Of course, present trends do not always predict the future. Furthermore, people making up cultural groups are not always alike. Hispanics are not identical in their politics and religion, nor are Asians, African Americans, or any other racial or ethnic group. Many Asians, when it comes to political issues, are more like some whites and Hispanics than they are like large numbers of people from Far Eastern countries. Furthermore, there is a great deal of intermarriage occurring. Hence, it would be wrong to hold to the myth that each of these groups is highly cohesive in all respects. But they do have shared cultural traditions, and they are struggling to find a balance between these traditions and what social scientists call "modernity." They are all struggling with biculturality—the task of relating to modernity while retaining enduring values from tradition. Some are also struggling to balance bilinguality, i.e., the memory of Spanish, Japanese, Korean, Chinese, or Tamil, with their efforts to learn English.

With these introductory definitions and clarifications in mind, we move to a consideration of the wider significance of our major point—that finding consensus on family issues entails taking seriously and working with, not against, our various cultural traditions.

2

Family, Tradition,
and Critique

Aconsensus on family issues can best occur if we first take
seriously the major cultural and religious traditions that
have shaped, and still are shaping, American society. These
traditions do not always agree, but there are analogies between their different views of marriage and family. These
analogies can constitute the grounds for a rough consensus.
In turn, these traditions must learn to cooperate with government, market, and other parts of civil society on family issues. This view is easy to write down in black and white, but
it is challenging to implement. Furthermore, it is not how
our society has always proceeded in practice.

The Role of the Social Sciences

Some of you must be asking: what is the role of the social
sciences such as psychology, sociology, and economics in establishing a consensus? Don't they have an important place
in the mix? After all, we send our young people to colleges
and universities. Who teaches the courses they take on marriage and family? For the most part, sociologists teach these

courses. Sometimes psychologists get involved, and more recently economists have become interested in the family. So,
aren't scholars from these disciplines the real experts on
family matters?

They most certainly are experts, and they have much to
contribute to developing a public philosophy on family matters. But the social sciences should not be the only participants in the great social dialogue required to develop a
public philosophy. This is a delicate point. Be assured that
the authors of this book in no way want to deprecate the
role of the social sciences in clarifying family issues. But we
do have a rather major point to make about their appropriate role. The point is this: there is no way to move directly
from the facts of social science research to a public philosophy about families. One can collect all the scientific data in
the world about families—and the very best data at that—
and not be able to derive from them even a rough consensus
about how to respond to the challenges facing families.
Thoughtful people know and understand this truth, but it is
easy to forget. All of us learn so much from the social sciences that we are tempted to think that they can give us the
really big answers.

Many of us learned in our college philosophy course an
insight relevant to this point. How many times did you hear
the professor say, "You can't derive an *ought* from an *is*."[4] It
sounded abstract and irrelevant, but the principle was highly
pertinent to how a consensus, and the norms governing a
consensus, is developed. Much social science seems to work
on the assumption that to develop a public philosophy and
policy, one must forget one's traditions and the values they
carry and turn solely to the facts. The facts alone, some believe, will themselves imply a philosophy. Many people think
that traditions don't count anymore; only science counts.
They assume that the data, the facts, and the measurements
of conditions and consequences will sooner or later give us
norms, tell us what we should do, and mediate our conflicts
over how to proceed. Some philosophers of science call this
a "foundationalist" theory of the role of science in social de-

liberations.[5] Whatever this view is called, it has been the object in recent years of serious philosophical criticism. Many philosophers do not think this approach works for the development of either normative ethics or public philosophy. We agree. Furthermore, we do not think that foundationalism, i.e., the move from empirical facts to positive norms, will ever work.

Our view is just the opposite. To develop consensus about anything, the parties involved have to understand their own beginning points very well, better than they do when they are not struggling to find agreement. Much misunderstanding and conflict comes when disputing groups do not understand well their own respective traditions. Western family patterns that affect culture, law, religion, and associated sensibilities took centuries to develop as did the family patterns from other backgrounds. In the Western tradition, they resulted from the interaction of general visions of life, moral reason, accumulated insights based on experience, and understandings of the facts of our human nature and social circumstances. Sometimes these traditions got the facts wrong, but more often they possessed amazing insights into the actual conditions of human nature and social reality.

Perceptions of the facts, however, never completely dictated the development of these traditions, and the facts alone will not determine our common view of the present and future on any issue, let alone family issues. To pretend that facts by themselves can produce agreement only ends in alienating us from our traditions.[6] Or even further, if the contemporary social sciences are used to dictate agreement about family issues independently of inherited traditions, this would end in offending, if not infuriating, huge sectors of our society who still think that they gain insight from their customs.

If tradition is so important in coming to understand family ideals and family patterns, what role is played by the social sciences? Our answer is this: they help clarify conflicts within and between traditions about how to interpret the facts of human nature and the social and cultural conditions that shape family life. Disputes over such facts and conditions emerge even within particular traditions, and the social sciences can help clarify them. But the social sciences as such cannot invent or create a tradition about family ideals and patterns. Hence, the social science disciplines must work within, not independently of, the deeper traditions that have shaped our cultural life.

In taking this position, we are not assuming a maverick stand. Works in the philosophy of the social sciences by such diverse academic fields as the English school of ordinary language analysis, continental phenomenology and hermeneutic philosophy, American pragmatism, and the fashionable schools of deconstructionism have all criticized the pretensions of foundationalism.[7] If you want reasonably good descriptions and facts, turn to the social sciences; if you want norms and consensus, begin with the traditions that have shaped our ideals. Quite clearly, however, we need both—the critical retrieval of our traditions and, secondly, good social science information and clarification. Traditions give us orientation, norms, and values; they creep into our experience even before we start thinking about them or actively interpreting them. The social sciences help us gain "distance," to use a phrase from Paul Ricoeur, from our inherited traditions. But distance and objectivity, without some sense of "belonging" to a culture and tradition, are alienating and finally confusing. In what follows, we plan to give the reader a taste of what we mean by tradition. This will be followed by some of the distance, description, and explanation of family trends that social science provides. Finally, we will return, with our eyes sharpened by the sciences, for a bit of criticism of tradition.

A more concrete example might help make our point. For instance, Rodriguez is more conservative on abortion than Browning. Knowing this, we could think that we must disagree with each other on everything pertaining to families. How can a Roman Catholic agree with a liberal Protestant about divisive family issues? If we stopped there, however, we would be making a serious mistake. We would

be eliminating from discussion a wide range of very important matters about which we might discover more common
ground—issues about the role of marriage in family formation, the importance of fathers, or the status of children.
And indeed, if the two of us search back into our respective
histories and the traditions that formed us, we will find
common sources that are easy to overlook if we take too
simplistic an understanding of the simple polarities of
Protestant-midwestern versus Catholic-southwestern. We
would find that our respective heritages have been shaped
by a common use of the scriptural classics of Genesis I and
II, the strong emphasis on mutual consent in marriage that
arose from the synthesis of Judeo-Christian and Roman-law
insights found in Catholic canon law, and the emphasis on
marriage as a public act that developed in the Reformation
and then in Catholicism after the Council of Trent.[8] And
this common heritage is not just shared by the two of us; it
is part of the implicit experience of most individuals living
within Western institutions. This is so whether they know it
explicitly or simply absorb these marriage and family traditions implicitly through interaction with the legal and cultural institutions that have shaped their lives. The two of us
make these points not in the mode of religious confession
but in the spirit of philosophical awareness about the classic
historical sources that have shaped our respective normative understandings of marriage and family.

Common Values and the Traditions

If we were to take our various cultural and religious traditions a bit more seriously, here are some of the main themes
that a public philosophy on families would develop.

1. Marriage would be viewed as integrally related to family
   formation and childbearing.

2. Marriage would be seen as not only a civil contract, although it certainly would be seen as at least that. Our society would as well, even in its public philosophy, honor

and find social space for the many ways marriage has been conceived as a sacred reality, i.e., a self-transcending reflection of the fundamental rhythms of reality (Confucianism), a covenant (Judaism, Protestantism), a sacrament (Catholicism, Hinduism), and a civil contract located within the framework of God's will (Islam).

3. Residential fathers would be seen as important to the well-being of children, and every effort would be made to socialize men to be responsible and help them continue as involved fathers even if their marriages fail or never develop.

4. Children would be highly valued, beyond their instrumental or economic usefulness.

5. Children would be viewed as needing not only material resources and education but the *presence and unconditioned affirmation* of parents, extended family, and the wider society. They would be viewed as needing a sense of identity provided by some religiocultural tradition stretching back into the past.

6. Poor families would be both supported and enabled, not only for the health of society but because of their intrinsic human worth.

7. Both men and women, husbands and wives, would be viewed as persons of equal worth.

8. It follows from the above affirmations that work and family issues must be freshly addressed in our kind of society. All sectors of society (churches, government, market, families) should cooperate to permit both husbands and wives, fathers and mothers, to participate freely in both market and domestic responsibilities without having their humanity totally consumed by the demands and logics of the market.

These principles give expression to a series of intrinsic values that resist the commodification and instrumentalization of life. The marital bond, the value of children, the respect for both husband and wife, and the dignity of the poor are all examples of realities that are good in themselves and not simply means to other ends. Religiocultural traditions, in different ways, inject a language of intrinsic values into our speech and thought. This provides a ground for commitment in family relations that exceeds much of the utilitarian language of the social sciences being used today to justify marriage and family. We offer these principles as *starting points, strong assumptions, or highly settled presumptions that society and culture have depended on in the past and, for that reason, they should have the status of likely guidelines for today.*[9]

To start with the assertion of the importance of marriage for families is not always popular in our present society. To connect family formation and childbearing with marriage, as we do, is even more controversial. Fathers? Well, they are nice, but are they really all that important if alternative economic resources are available? The social sciences spend a great deal of time calculating the cost and benefits of a father's presence and absence. But what do our religious and cultural traditions say about fathers and fatherhood? What presumptions have these traditions shaped in our consciousness about the role and importance of fathers? It is our thesis that we should, indeed, listen to these traditions as well as to the social sciences.

And what about children? Are they important? Economists tell us that in our kind of society, children are becoming less important. Why? They have less economic or instrumental value; they cost a lot, require a great deal of energy and labor, and do not contribute to the family wealth as they once did in agricultural societies. Furthermore, children today for the most part do not take care of us when we get old.[10] They get in the way of self-actualization and enjoyment. So why have them? Indeed, that question is increasingly being answered in the negative, as birth rates drop below replacement in many Western societies. Economists tell us that when contemporary couples are faced with the choice between a child and a late model automobile, they increasingly select the shiny new car. How, on the other hand, have our religious and cultural traditions spoken about the value of a child? And how have they located the good of children within the total framework of the goods of life? For instance, even today, not all communities are following the predictions of the economists. To illustrate, the fertility rate for Hispanics in the U.S. is 3.0 but only 1.8 for whites. Many Hispanics believe this is because their traditions have taught them to value children, even in the midst of declining economic fortunes and a surrounding culture with lower birth rates. Although Hispanic families have average incomes slightly higher than blacks (in 1995 $22,393 for blacks, $22,860 for Hispanics), a higher percentage of Hispanics than blacks is now below the poverty line.[11] According to economists, children don't pay, but Hispanics want them anyway. Furthermore, even though many Hispanics are poor, the mortality rate of their children is low. They care for their children in spite of poverty. Our thesis here is this: culture counts.

We do not need to complete here our commentary on the above list of affirmations to make our central point: the utilitarian, economic, and material analyses of families typical of most of the social sciences, as important as they are, both marginalize tradition and lose the richness of some of our classic ways of speaking about family matters. To gain a rough consensus on family matters and to create a public philosophy on family issues, we need both the language of traditions and the language of the social sciences, with the social science language clarifying and sometimes critiquing, but not replacing, the languages of tradition.

The Criticism and Reconstruction of Tradition

But the great traditions that we have inherited, as full of wisdom as they are on family issues, are not always totally relevant to the challenges of modern and postmodern life. Most everything from the past, even if it is appreciated and largely retained, often needs criticism and reformulation.[12] There are two ways to do this. One way is to impose on these traditions values that we believe (sometimes mistakenly) are totally modern. For instance, many believe that the ideas of justice, human dignity, freedom, and human rights were invented by liberal social philosophies of the Enlightenment or perhaps only during the twentieth century.[13] For people who hold that point of view, the criticism of tradition entails imposing modern ideas on the outdated ideas of the past.

But there is another point of view about how traditions are revised. This view believes that many great traditions often contain within them normative insights that became distorted or forgotten but that can be rediscovered and used to critique and revise the questionable practices that have become attached to the classic tradition. One does not have to believe that this is *always* the case in order to hold that it is *often* the case. This point of view would say that our images of justice and human dignity were not simply invented by modern societies; the seeds of these ideals were embedded in the great traditions of the past. In addition, they were often placed within larger narratives about the meaning and purpose of life that endowed these implicit theories of justice and human rights with additional energy and force.

But this discussion is too abstract. Some examples will help. It is widely believed today that nearly all cultural and religious traditions from the past are either mildly or profoundly patriarchal. There is some truth in this allegation. This means that they in principle or reality subordinated women to the authority of men. It also means that these traditions often used the authority of sacred scriptures and religious symbols to legitimate this subordination. There is some truth in that view as well. Let's face it: every culture and society in antiquity was patriarchal. Truly primitive cultures may have been more egalitarian. Cultures that are basically subsistence societies, built around hunting animals for protein and gathering berries, nuts, vegetables, and fruits, may have been far less patriarchal. But as herding and agriculture developed and inheritable property began to accumulate, certain kinds of power increasingly fell into the hands of males. In these societies, social systems were patriarchal. Both culture and religion reflected it and, yes, often legitimized it.

But the religion of these patriarchal societies often contained deeper insights that constrained the power of men and enhanced the status of women. These deeper insights are seen in their founding documents and can be retrieved by sound interpretation and used as critical leverages for the needs of today. *Hence, the criticism of traditions need not always come from the outside; often it can be developed from the inner resources of these traditions themselves, thereby keeping them intact and helping them to evolve with more integrity and cohesion.*

This brings us to the major point of this chapter. The family wisdom of many cultural and religious traditions needs to be criticized and reformulated with regard to the understanding of male authority and male responsibility. But this criticism can often come from within the traditions themselves. Many classic traditions—Judaism, Catholicism, Protestantism, Islam, Hinduism—emphasized and reinforced ideals of male responsibility to wife, children, and community. In addition, however, founding leaders and documents often emphasized the equal dignity and treatment of women. Some scholars of Judaism believe that Genesis 1:27 asserts that male and female are made equally in the image of God.[14] Scholarship shows that the Buddha taught the fundamental dignity of women through his teachings on the emptiness and co-arising of all reality. Mohammed, we now know, was progressive on women's rights in relation to the culture of his day and the Arabic cultures that succeeded him. Early Christianity elevated the status of women, especially when measured against the honor-shame codes of the Greco-Roman world that surrounded it. And even Hinduism, often considered one of the most restrictive for women, has a more elevated place for women in its classical scriptures.

But many of these traditions did not carry through in developing these early insights. They often linked male responsibility with male leadership, authority, and control. This gave rise to *nomic* patriarchy, i.e., a principled patriarchy that uses the prerogatives of authority to enhance the exercise of responsibility. This must be contrasted with *anomic* patri-

archy where male authority is used in self-serving and irresponsible ways—ways that are destructive to wife, children,
and finally even to the wider community.

Aristotle gave us the classic articulation of nomic patriarchy when he characterized in his *Nicomachean Ethics* and
Politics the relation of husband to wife as a matter of aristocratic rule. He thought this rule was analogous to the gover-
nance of a ruler over his subjects, when the latter have at
least *some* constitutional rights. He further characterized the
relation of a father to his children as monarchical rule in
analogy, once again, to the rule of a king to subjects who
have *no* constitutional rights. In both cases, Aristotle taught
that a father should use his aristocratic and monarchical authority for the good of the wife and children. He should do
that in ways similar to a just and powerful king who is self-
sufficient and "needs nothing further; therefore he will not
look to his own interests but to those of his subjects." Nomic
patriarchy was ideally quite benevolent and responsible, but
it was also paternalistic and could easily become arbitrary.

Patriarchy has been on the decline for hundreds of years
in Western societies. In law, work, and politics, women
enjoy a great deal of formal freedom and equality, although this is not fully realized in practice. Many modern
societies are evolving toward what we in this book call "the
equal regard marriage and family." But our society is not
quite there. Furthermore, just as there is a difference between nomic and anomic patriarchy, there is a distinction
between nomic and anomic equality in gender relations,
both within and outside of marriage. It is possible for a
husband and wife to be equal, but also *equally irresponsible.*
There is the possibility of defining equality in marriage in
such a way as to achieve very few dependencies between
husband and wife, to have very limited obligations, and for
both husband and wife to be equally free to walk away from
the other and their children if things are not to their satisfaction. Since men are less burdened by pregnancy and the
struggles of childbirth, anomic equality may end by being a
worse deal for wives and mothers than it is for husbands

and fathers. It may even be a worse deal for mothers and children than was nomic patriarchy.

The Equal Regard Marriage and Family

Our task for today, then, is to understand and respect the remnants of nomic patriarchy for what it represented about male responsibility to families. As we said above, patriarchy has been declining for centuries and has become increasingly weak and pallid. Yet destructive forms of it still exist, even in the liberal and progressive West. And there is a good deal of ambivalent, erratic, and anomic patriarchy still in existence. *The cultural reconstructive task of our time is to preserve, honor, and appreciate the element of male responsibility that was sometimes associated with the paternalisms of the past but now couple this responsibility with a new ethic of "equal regard."* This ethic of equal regard can often be found, as we suggested above, in the deeper strands of a particular tradition; it does not always need to be imported from the outside—from the Enlightenment or other modern philosophies. An ethic of equal regard is a way of defining love in families. It defines love as equal respect; but it also defines it as equal effort by both husband and wife to work for the good—the welfare— of the other. It is concerned with issues of equal justice and fairness. But love as equal regard is also concerned to convert the passion that led a couple to marry into concrete behaviors balancing between them the privileges and responsibilities of both public and domestic life.

These words about a love ethic of equal regard may make the reader uncomfortable. Some will say, "This kind of thinking is the province of religion or private conviction and not the stuff of public philosophy and public policy." We think it can be the concern of both religion *and* public philosophy. There is more than one way to ground an ethic of mutual respect and equal regard. Some people might turn to the doctrine of the *imago Dei* (the idea that all humans are made in the image of God) shared by Judaism and Christianity. Islam believes that this dignity is assigned to humans

by God. Some people might anchor an ethic of mutual respect in a Kantian understanding of the rationality of all humans and thereby their right to be treated as persons—as
ends and never a means only. No matter which way one
might justify this ethic, we believe it is suitable for guiding a
public philosophy for marriage and families. It is precisely
this kind of ethic that should guide the education of youth
preparing for marriage and family, the organization of work
and family life, the policies governing the taxation of families, the organization of health insurance, the issue of which
parent might take part in family leave policies, and many
other such issues.

Many parts of our society are interested in what we call
the equal regard marriage and family. Sociologist Pepper
Schwartz has investigated a similar concept in her 1994
book titled *Peer Marriage*. Legal scholar Amy Wax has used
the idea in her writings. A joint statement titled "The Marriage Movement: A Statement of Principles" designed to
provide a philosophy for the emerging efforts to strengthen
the marital institution also used the equal regard concept to
describe the kind of marriage it was promoting.[15] University
of Virginia sociologist Steven Nock has developed a new
"normative model of marriage" that emphasizes gender
equality as the core ideal.[16] An empirical study reported in
the summary book of the Religion, Culture, and Family Project of the University of Chicago found that a majority of
Americans think that a good marriage correlates with love
defined as mutuality or equal regard as opposed to either
love as sheer self-sacrifice *or* love as self-fulfillment. Fifty-five
percent thought that a good marriage was likely to entail a
relation of mutuality; only 38 percent thought it was mainly
built on self-sacrifice by one or both members of the couple.
Only 5 percent thought that a good marriage correlated
with love defined as self-fulfillment. When respondents were
asked what they thought their parents believed, it was just
the reverse. Adults today think their parents idealized self-
sacrifice far more than mutuality or equal regard. And they
believe that their mothers idealized the role of self-sacrifice

in a good marriage more than their fathers (56 percent for the mothers and only 40 percent for their fathers).[17] Sociologists Frances Goldscheider and Linda Waite asked an ominous question in their 1991 book titled *New Families, No Families?* The implication is that *new* families, because of the extensive involvement in the wage market by both husband and wife, must begin to work out the issues of equal responsibilities or, indeed, there increasingly will be *no* families. Without further cultural progress toward the equal regard marriage, more nonmarriage, divorce, and family violence may be typical of the future even more than is the case today.

So there is a great deal of interest in what we call the equal regard marriage and family. This raises the question: *do people today know how to achieve the kind of marriage and family that most of them want and that new economic realities seem to demand?* Does our society know how to create such a human reality? Do parents, schools, churches, businesses, the professions, and government know what to do on their own or in cooperation with other parts of society to create this new institution? Do the traditions have something to contribute or are they an obstacle? Do we even know how to define such an institution or what it would look like in the concrete?

There are two understandings of the equal regard marriage. One sees it in analogy to partners with equal power negotiating a business contract to their mutual advantage. This is virtually the way legal scholar Amy Wax defines the equal regard marriage; it is a marriage in which "each partner 'gets his or her way' to a similar degree within the relationship or alternatively, that each gains an equal amount of net 'utility' or overall benefit." For Wax, the equal regard marriage is one arrived at through a bargain, maybe even through *Hard Bargains,* to borrow a phrase from the title of a 1998 book by legal scholars Linda Hirschman and Jane Larson. From a philosophical point of view, both of these positions should be seen as ethical-egoist views of moral obligation in marriage. Marriage is viewed as a contract that

contributes to the individual good of each of the members
of the couple. If individual advantage is not being increased,
and if repeated negotiations do not improve the situation,
then the contract should be broken. This is love viewed as
an instrument of individual fulfillment, a view of marriage,
according to the study referred to above, that only 5 percent
of Americans believe correlates with a good marriage. Yet it
is a view highly popular with many legal scholars and social
scientists.

The second definition of the equal regard marriage is
based on a deeper understanding of the role of mutual respect for the dignity and selfhood of the other. In fact, this
second view of the equal regard marriage assumes a cognitive and moral conversion on the part of each member of
the marital partnership. Maybe this is what a public wedding
ceremony is all about: it symbolizes and stabilizes a conversion from self-regard to equal regard. In this view, the conversion goes something like this: "I will respect your dignity
and selfhood as profoundly as I do my own, and furthermore, I will work for your welfare as seriously as I do my
own. I also expect you to respect me and work equally for
my welfare." The first formulation of equal regard is conditional; it says, "I will love and help you *if* you love and help
me." The second is nonconditional; it says, "In marrying
you, I pledge to love and assist you *as fully* as I am inclined to
regard myself, and to do this independently of moment-to-
moment reciprocity." There is a profound difference between these two definitions of love as equal regard.

As the lives of American men and women get more and
more entangled in the conditional and cost-benefit logics of
the marketplace, we are also more inclined to think of our
love and marriage relationships like business contracts, i.e.,
like conditional forms of equal regard. Public philosophy
should not lose the deeper grounds that our religious traditions provide for respecting self, other, and child. One need
not argue like a witnessing or confessing Jew, Christian, Muslim, or Hindu to make this broader philosophical point, i.e.,
that the equal regard marriage may require deep apprecia-

tion for the dignity and value of both self and other and that the languages of these traditions have often provided the deeper, more sacred grounds for this affirmation. The equal regard marriage as we define it certainly entails some bargaining and negotiation but within the context of a prior *commitment* to the equal value and dignity of both self and other.

Tradition and Commitment

We end this chapter with a slice of experience that comes from the life of one of us. It illustrates the power and importance of healthy traditions. Gloria Rodriguez's grandmother and father first settled in Zuehl, Texas, as sharecroppers before moving to San Antonio. Her mother's parents had also crossed the Mexican border and eventually moved to San Antonio. Her father was Mexican with Spanish roots, and her mother was indigenous Indian with Mexican roots. In spite of poverty and lack of education, this family had a cultural identity and family cohesion that led them to gradually flourish in the new country. When young people married, they tried to stay close to their parents and grandparents. Both grandmothers and grandfathers played important leadership roles for the two succeeding generations—their children and their grandchildren—as is the case in Hispanic culture in general. The Roman Catholicism of their families gave Gloria and her husband Salvador a strong pro-family and pro-marriage ethic that guided them into strong adult marriage and family relationships. Grandparents, uncles, aunts, and a strong community of neighbors provided an endless source of practical helpfulness but also a veritable bevy of positive role models, stories, and tales about family, cultural, and religious heroes. She acknowledges that there was some *machismo* that needed critique and that was probably not even consistent with more authentic strands of her Roman Catholic and Aztec traditions. Furthermore, mothers may have converted too frequently their love and care into *la sacrificada,* a self-sacrificial love that sometimes became an end in itself rather than a balance and restoration of love as equal regard. This too needs critique but not in a manner that would undercut the responsibility to marriage, family, and parenting that she found so widespread in the Hispanic community she knew as a child.

There is no doubt that the forces of modernization in many ways work against family cohesion of this kind; but it is also true that such strong family traditions also help individuals weather the storms of modernization and handle them with greater skills. This illustrates what we meant by asserting that a consensus on family issues should build on and appreciate—not by-pass and ignore—the positive cultural and religious traditions that have shaped American life.

3

Is Family Disruption Real?

What is unique about our central argument? If we believe that consensus on family issues is best achieved by taking our cultural and religious traditions seriously—instead of ignoring them—what does this mean in relation to other prevalent strategies for gaining agreement? Identifying the alternatives will make our views clearer.

Our Strategy Contrasted with Others

First, many contemporary policy makers believe that consensus will occur when all people get involved more and more in the modernizing process. The modernization process, they believe, itself makes us more alike and produces agreement. Modernization is the quest for ever more efficient means to satisfy our human wants and desires. The technological employment of science to achieve more efficient production, management, mobility, and speed of communication is the central characteristic of the modernization process. The great German economist and sociologist Max Weber described modernization as the ascendency over all

human activity of technical reason—the increase of powerful
and efficient means-end procedures for realizing our everyday wants. Sooner or later, he believed, the unrestricted use
of technical reason would place all of modern civilization
into an "iron cage."[18] Whether this has happened—whether
we have placed ourselves into the hard constraints of a technological prison—is an issue cultural critics are presently debating.

However this issue is settled, many people would say that
the modernizing process homogenizes our families. It does
so by making families less important, subordinating them to
the ambitions and wants of the individuals in them, rendering them more fragile, assigning them less significance for
determining our status, and making them more or less irrelevant to our ability to fit the work roles of modern industry.
In modern societies, some sociologists tell us, people are defined by what they do in an institutional system; they are less
and less defined by their families or whether they even have
one.[19] Modernization causes people to become increasingly
functional and anonymous; it tends to reduce individuals
and families to the requirements of social efficiency and to
encourage mobility, consumerism, and separation from kin.
This view says families will become more alike—and thereby
find consensus—because they will gradually forget their distinctive cultural and religious traditions and become ho-
mogenized into the universal functional roles of advanced
industrial and technological societies. This view would de-
ride the thesis of this book, i.e., that consensus comes by
working through traditions rather than by evading them. For-
getting our traditions will almost certainly lead us all to become totally absorbed into the spreading cost-benefit logics
associated with the new union between technology and the
market. It is tempting to choose the path of liberation from
our respective religious and cultural traditions, but it almost
surely means that we will become captured instead by the
iron links being forged between technical rationality and
the market. We might achieve unanimity, but with a price.

There is a second view that is also quite different from

the one that we propose in this book. This position holds that people increasingly will become more individualistic as modernization proceeds. They will become interested in their individual fulfillment—their own self-actualization, satisfactions, and enjoyments. This will lead to heightened rates of family disruption, marital failure, and an emerging culture of nonmarriage. Families will become more alike because they will share increasingly in their mutual broken-ness. Family disruption itself will be the grounds for a new family consensus. This is what Jan Dizard and Howard Gadlin predict in their provocative *The Minimal Family* (1990). In this situation, government programs should provide the needed new family supports; indeed, state bureaucracies should meet the emerging needs, dependencies, and vulnerabilities of disrupted families in order to keep them from falling through the social cracks. Families, according to this view, cannot be strengthened; they can only be assisted. And cultural and religious traditions that once functioned to define and support families will, for the most part, become too weak to do much good. Indeed, this view ignores the entire field of civil society as a constructive and helpful resource and turns completely to the power and efficiency of bureaucratic initiatives, which often in fact are fragmented and unconnected to the traditions of the people they serve.

There is a third strategy, one that at first glance might look like the one proposed in this book. In reality, it is quite different. This view says that the traditions—primarily the Christian tradition—should provide the basis of the new consensus. This position, advocated by some but not all of the Christian Right, believes that Judaism and Christianity provided much of the cultural and legal resources for defining family in the West. These religions also provided the means for socializing individuals into a stable understanding of the meaning of marriage.[20] This view wants to bring much of the Judeo-Christian tradition back not only to churches and individuals but also to government policies and the law courts.

The authors of this book differ with this position in several respects. We believe that proponents of this third perspective have every right to express and argue for their point of view. Furthermore, they are correct in assuming that Judaism, Roman Catholicism, and the Protestant Reformation contributed massively to the development of Western cultural and legal patterns pertaining to marriage and family They are also correct that these contributions were, for the most part, efficacious. We will try to show that later.

So, where do they go wrong? Their mistake is the failure to recognize the complexity of the Judeo-Christian tradition on marriage and family, how it from the beginning was mixed with other perspectives (Jewish theology and law, Roman Hellenism, Roman law, German law, etc.)[21] and how today what is valid about this synthesis must be submitted to the tests of public debate. If much of this tradition has validity, it cannot be given credibility—as far as public debate is concerned—simply because it *is* Christian as such, but because it can be seen to contain wisdom and make good sense for a more general public philosophy. The error of the Christian Right is not in holding its views or offering them to the public arena. Its misstep is relying too much on rhetoric and failing to argue its positions well, openly, and honestly with a frank confrontation of the complexity of the present pluralistic situation and, indeed, the full complexity of the tradition they promote. The Christian Right invokes tradition and in this sense is traditionalistic. But there is little evidence that it carefully studies tradition.

Hence, to argue, as we do, that consensus comes by taking traditions seriously, but yet critiquing them, is a different point of view. Furthermore, our view assumes that various traditions can, if they try hard enough, make intelligible public arguments. This too is different from the Christian Right. In addition, to say that traditions must enter into a complex dialogue with government, market, and other parts of civil society is also distinctive. These points make up our position. But to make our perspective convincing, we must come up with additional arguments and illustrations.

Before we take on this task, we must ask: *is there really a family problem?* Has the so-called family crisis been manufactured, invented, and fabricated for devious and sinister political and economic reasons? Furthermore, if the so-called family crisis is real, what are its causes? Cures must fit diagnoses. If our society is confronted by a real social illness, how would our solutions fit the causes?

Evidence that the Family Crisis Is Real

We believe that there is a real family crisis. But there are also positive family gains. It is better to start with the positive before dwelling on the negative. On the affirmative side of the ledger, we believe that we must list the greater freedom of women. Family changes in the last century have given women higher levels of education, greater participation in political activity, and much wider participation in the wage economy. Immeasurable amounts of talent and energy have been unleashed into the public realm; incalculable treasures of "human capital" (to use the phrase of Nobel prize–winning economist Gary Becker) have been deposited on behalf of the public. If this means that women have joined men and become too deeply engulfed in the all-consuming pursuit of wealth, power, and fame in the ever-spreading market, then the problem may be more a matter of their excess involvement rather than the sheer fact of their participation in this sector of society. And if this is the problem, then it can be addressed by taking concrete steps to lower everyone's involvement—both males and females—in the wage economy. We will make specific recommendations to this effect later in the book.

There is the positive factor of improved education, not only for women in general, but for fathers and mothers as well as their children. Improved education correlates with improved health, income, and capacities for communication. These are all conditions that improve family life. All are real pluses and must not be ignored. These advances even serve to balance, to a certain extent, the negative forces and consequences that we will discuss below. But a good education and income do not solve all the problems facing families, partially because not all families have these things. In addition, some poor and relatively uneducated families are surprisingly strong in their relationships, their sense of belonging, and their attachments to a wider community.

Children

Family disruption has been costly to several groups in our society. It has been costly to children. Here are some facts from a few of the more recent and authoritative studies. After analyzing four national studies of families, three of which were longitudinal, Sara McLanahan and Gary Sandefur in their *Growing up with a Single Parent* (1994) concluded with stunning directness that

Children who grow up in a household with only one biological parent are worse off, on average, than children who grow up in the household with both of their biological parents, regardless of the parent's race or educational background, regardless of whether the parents are married when the child is born, and regardless of whether the resident parent remarries.

To be more specific, their data indicate that children whose parents live apart are twice as likely to drop out of high school, one and a half times as likely to be unemployed when they are young adults, and two times more likely to become single parents themselves. Race and income make a difference in the statistics, but they do not alter them completely. For instance, "For the white children, family disruption eliminates the advantage of being white with respect to high school graduation." Income—especially a sudden loss of income—also makes a difference, but after education, residence, race, and number of siblings are taken into account, income only cuts these rates by one half. It must be pointed out that these rates, as arresting as they are, should not be used to obscure the fact that the children of many single parents do well. But, at the same time, these rates should not be ignored. Indeed, similar rates predicting chances for getting lung cancer, having heart attacks, or experiencing kidney failure would not be ignored.

The respected work of Paul Amato and Alan Booth in *A Generation at Risk: Growing up in an Era of Family Upheaval* (1997) says much the same thing. Single parenthood, whether by divorce or nonmarital births, has on average negative effects on children. But so does poor marital quality. In fact, from their perspective, this is the crucial factor. They write:

> If marital quality is no lower now than it was thirty years ago, then the positive and negative trends of the last three decades may well have balanced one another, leaving children no worse off, but no better. Yet larger social trends, as well as a handful of studies, suggest that marital quality is declining. If this is true, then the balance for offspring making the transition to adulthood has tilted in a negative direction. Unless marriage becomes a more satisfying and secure arrangement in the future, the outlook for future generations of youth may be even more pessimistic.

Amato and Booth believe that divorce on average has negative effects on children. Nonmarital births leading to single parenthood have adverse consequences as well. But what does it mean to say that poor marital quality also has bad effects? Does this imply that it is better for children if parents divorce rather than endure a low-quality marriage? That conclusion, it appears, would be premature. Amato and Booth argue that "less than a third of parental divorces involve highly conflicted marriages," i.e., marriages marred by "physical abuse" or regular and "serious quarrels." Two-thirds of divorces occur in low-conflict families. In view of these figures, they conclude that divorce may be beneficial for children in high-conflict marriages but not for the majority of children who in fact come from low-conflict unions. They conclude that the high rate of divorce in both kinds of marriage has, on balance, been detrimental to children. Furthermore, if the threshold of marital unhappiness required to trigger a divorce continues to decline, then outcomes for children of divorced parents may become more problematic in the future.

This last piece of information, not completely without controversy, has startling implications for a national public philosophy on families. It suggests that many divorces may truly be unnecessary. The conflict in many marriages may be of the kind that could be prevented or corrected with good premarital education, good postmarriage education, and good community and mentoring supports that model commitment. These data pose the possibility that current divorce trends are not inevitable and that our society conceivably might learn to live in marriages and families more positively in spite of the strains and struggles of modern life. And, if lowering the divorce rate is a genuine possibility, then the massive negative impact of divorce on many children might be lessened. Those who are pessimists about changing the family trends of the last several decades may just be wrong.

Husbands and Fathers

If divorce and nonmarital births are not, on average, good for children, what does this imply for the role of fathers? Is the presence of fathers in the lives of their children really necessary? Is father absence a problem, or are other facts such as poverty, the social isolation of single mothers and their children, inadequate community support, or the sheer lack of time and energy of the custodial parent the real problems—not father absence as such? Several contemporary commentators minimize the importance of the actual residential presence of fathers.[22] They contend that if the lost earning power of the father is replaced, the social isolation of mother and child is overcome, or additional help is found, the father is not all that important.

There is little doubt that sufficient money and social capital in the form of friends, organizations, and extended family can be of enormous help to single mothers and their children. Certain functions performed by any parent—father or mother—can to some extent be replaced—especially by grandparents, uncles, and aunts. But fathers are important, first as husbands, helpers, and companions to mothers. Research shows that on average having a husband lowers stress and depression.[23] But there is also growing empirical evidence that fathers as such make a positive difference for children. Amato, Popenoe, Snarey, and McLanahan and Sandefur have all made powerful arguments that the moral, cognitive, and psychological contributions of fathers to their children cannot be easily replaced.[24] Take education. It is often thought that father absence is harder on boys than girls, but the evidence suggests, as McLanahan and Sandefur write, that living without the father's presence "may have a more negative effect on girls than on boys," and the school dropout rates for girls headed by a single mother are from 3 to 6 percentages points higher than that for boys from these families, depending on the study. We are fully aware that there is a significant debate over whether programs addressing the absence of poor fathers from their children should promote marriage or simply encourage father involvement by providing peer help, skills training, job training, and other nonpunitive encouragements.[25] We will review this debate in more detail later. Suffice it to say now that we do not believe it is a contradiction to emphasize both—father involvement as a first step but family formation and marriage when possible. To emphasize both, however, may mean that different spheres of society should play slightly different roles in promoting distinguishable but complementary cultural messages and social reinforcements.

Fathers may be important for children, but marriage and family life are also important for husbands and fathers. In fact, much contemporary social science research deals with the benefits of marriage for men. The fact that marriage generally entails children means that fatherhood must be part of the benefit of marriage for men. Sociologist Linda Waite of the University of Chicago delivered a groundbreaking lecture for her 1995 presidential address before the Population Association of America. This lecture and a recent book called *The Case for Marriage* (2000), co-authored with Maggie Gallagher, summarize the benefits of marriage for both men and women. Although the benefits for men slightly outweigh those for women, in general married couples have fewer difficulties with alcohol, have lower levels of risk taking, live longer, have more sex, have more satisfying sex, and accumulate more wealth than nonmarried individuals. There is an exception that pertains to the frequency of sex. Cohabiting couples do indeed have more sex, but it is also less personally satisfying. One possible explanation for why married couples acquire more wealth is that they may develop saving habits in planning for their children's future.

Sociologist Steven Nock of the University of Virginia has further documented the effects of marriage and parenthood on husbands and fathers. For instance, marriage is associated with higher levels of achievement for men. The transition into the institution of marriage and parenthood is accompanied by higher wages, longer working hours, and more prestigious positions. Indeed, married men become more socially involved and more generous; they give more of their resources to relatives and friends. This is true for more traditional marriages where men are generally thought to be the head of the family. But Nock believes that there will be measurable benefits for men in marriage and parenthood in the emerging "new normative marriage," a view of marriage that is similar to what we have called in this book the "equal regard marriage." The task of the new normative marriage, according to Nock, is to eliminate inequalities but not necessarily mutual dependencies. He believes that in the emerging new normative marriage where both husband and wife share in family leadership, income production, public involvement, parenting, and domestic chores, their mutual dependencies will actually increase. The couple will need each other all the more. This should also increase their mutual satisfactions.[26]

Such benefits for men of marriage and parenting are not restricted to middle- and upper-class men. Sociologists Laub, Nagin, and Sampson have shown that young men who have

broken the law and been involved with gangs often start living more responsible lives after they wed.[27] There is also evidence that higher degrees of responsibility in the sense of
higher incomes, more prestige, more achievement, and
more sharing are associated with having a child, especially if
this child comes within marriage.[28]

Wives and Mothers

We somehow naturally assume that mothers are good for
their children. When marital disruption occurs, mothers
generally in our society retain custody of the children. This
was not always the case in Western societies in earlier times,
and it does not always happen in other societies even today.
Our belief that mothers are essential for their children probably stems from deep intuitions that recently have been clar-
ified by the discipline of evolutionary psychology. Although
both fathers and mothers are invested equally in their offspring from the perspective of their respective gene contributions (50 percent of a child's genes come from each
parent), the mother's investment through carrying the
child, giving it birth, and nursing it in its early days certainly
exceeds the father's, even the most committed father. This
may be the reason that society's concern about child abuse
with some justification focuses on fathers. Nonetheless,
when mothers get overwhelmed, short of resources and
help, and isolated from other forms of what sociologist
James Coleman called "social capital," even they can become
abusive—hence, the high frequency of physical child abuse
from the hands of poor single mothers. Once again, it may
not be the single mothers themselves who are to blame as it
is the trying circumstances in which they find themselves—
their lack of psychological and communal supports.

Mothers may have a unique and demanding role to play
in situations of marital disruption. Recent research from the
University of Iowa throws new light on the role of the custodial parent, who is generally the mother. When all adverse
factors associated with family disruption are measured—loss

of income, parental conflict, parenting competence of the custodial parent, involvement of the father—this study shows that the parenting competence of *both* father and mother in the post-divorce situation can greatly reduce the ill effects on children. Nonetheless, the competence of the custodial parent, who is more often the mother, appears to be the weightier factor.[29] However, according to these researchers, even a competent mother with an involved nonresidential father does not remove the higher incidence of depression among boys that comes with divorce. Nor does it remove the fact that it is not easy to attain the high level of parenting competence needed to mitigate the negative consequences of divorce.

So, on the whole, father absence and stress on custodial mothers have negative effects on children. They also deprive mothers of the positive benefits of marriage. Remember, the summary of the positive values of marriage applies nearly as fully to women as men. Hence, women who are not married—and this certainly includes single mothers—have poorer health, die earlier, have less satisfying sex lives, and accumulate less wealth than married women. Furthermore, there is research showing that the loss of income by women after divorce ranges from between 30 and 47 percent, depending on the study.[30] All in all, it seems reasonable to conclude that divorce, nonmarital births, and the rising culture of nonmarriage are not an encouraging trend for either children, fathers, or mothers. For these and other reasons, these trends are not good for the wider society.

The Emerging Culture of Nonmarriage

Although there is evidence of the emergence, as Nock says, of a new normative image of marriage, there are also trends toward a new culture and reality of nonmarriage. Fewer people are getting married. In addition, more are getting married later, getting divorced, marrying a second time and divorcing again, and living longer periods of their lives in the single state. This is true even for those who are having children. Cohabitation is on the increase. Divorce rates doubled between 1960 and 1985. Although they have leveled off at slightly under 50 percent of all new marriages, this may in part be due to the increase in cohabitation.

Legal scholar Carl Schneider writes about the deinstitutionalization of marriage, i.e., the increase of relatively transient pairing and procreation outside legally contracted marital relations.[31] The scholars and family experts who make up the Council on Families in America have written about the emerging "culture of nonmarriage" and have called instead for a new "culture of marriage" and a "new familism."[32] As an alternative to the deinstitutionalization of marriage and family, The Religion, Culture, and Family Project located at the University of Chicago calls for a new "critical familism" and a "critical marriage culture," i.e., a new marriage culture that uncovers and critiques centers of power and resistance that function to block the development of the new normative or equal regard marriage and family.[33]

Can this critical familism and equal regard marriage provide a new ethic for future families? Can it constitute an attractive alternative to deinstitutionalization? There has been a substantial decrease in the number of traditional families—the classic industrial family of the nineteenth century marked by wage earning fathers and stay at home mothers. This family form has decreased from 53 percent in 1972 to 21 percent in 1998. On the other hand, the so-called modern family pattern, where both husband and wife work in the wage economy, has increased from 32 percent to 59 percent during the same period. We feel that both types of families need the love ethic of equal regard, but from the perspective of maintaining marital stability, the new dual-income family needs it even more profoundly. Since economic dependencies do not integrate these marriages like they do traditional ones, an ethic promoting equal dignity, responsibilities, and privileges is all the more important.

It is not surprising to learn, however, that people are delaying marriage, choosing it less, and leaving it at higher

rates. According to a recent report from the National Opinion Research Center, between 1960 and 1997 the median
age for first marriages rose from 22.8 to 26.8 years for men
and from 20.3 to 25 years for women. In addition, the newspapers have been full of reports about nonmarital births increasing from 5 percent in 1960 to 32 percent today. This
entails a huge ten-fold increase for whites, from around 2
percent in the early 1960s to over 32 percent today. This is
proportionately a far higher rate than the rise of nonmarital
births for African Americans, which climbed from 22 percent in 1960 to 70 percent today. Furthermore, the proportion of adults who have never been married increased from
15 percent to 23 percent between 1972 and 1998. Less marriage, more divorce, and more out-of-wedlock births—these
are the trends that point to the emerging deinstitutionalization of marriage and the rising culture of nonmarriage.

Perhaps, however, the systematic increase in the rate of
cohabitation is the key index of the new trend toward deinstitutionalization. Only 1.1 percent of couples cohabited in
1960; now 7 percent of all couples living together are cohabiting and thereby living outside legally sanctioned and
legally protected marriages. As Tom Smith of the National
Opinion Research Center says:

. . . for women born in 1933–1942 only 7% first lived with someone in
cohabitation rather than in a marriage, but for women born in
1963–1974, 64 percent started off cohabiting rather than marrying.
The trend for men is similar. Among the currently divorced, 16 percent are cohabiting and of those who have remarried 50 percent report cohabiting with their new spouse before their remarriage.[34]

Linda Waite reports that four million couples cohabit
today, "eight times as many as in 1970."[35] Cohabitation is
now widely affirmed—especially among young people—as a
socially acceptable transition into marriage with two-thirds
of them cohabiting first before marriage.

But recent research shows that cohabitation is an extremely fragile arrangement with most cohabiting couples
breaking up before marriage. Cohabitors on average share

less housework, generally do not combine their incomes, do not relate strongly to the surrounding community and to each other's families, often do not become involved in churches, are twice as likely to entail violence, are worse for children, and are much more likely to divorce if they do become married.[36] Although cohabitors have more frequent sex, they report less satisfaction with their sexual lives than do married couples. It is true that cohabitors possess certain personality characteristics that lead them to be less committed to their relationships (what sociologists call the "selection effect"). But it is also likely, as Waite and others argue, that the cohabiting "deal" itself—its tentativeness, its lack of publicly acknowledged and institutionally reinforced supports—"*causes* attitudes to change in ways inimical to long-term commitments." In many ways, then, cohabitation has negative consequences for both couples and the wider community.

This brief report of current trends tells us that reports of a family crisis have credibility. They are not a product of exaggeration although they are often overstated. They are not a product of social hysteria and not a figment of the cultural imagination. Marriage and family trends and the associated decline in child well-being have been subject to political manipulation by both the political right and the political left. But the manipulation itself has not created the problem of marriage and family; the issues surrounding increased family disruption are real and waiting to be more seriously addressed—by government, market, and the institutions of civil society.

4

Family Disruption: Diagnosis and the Search for a Cure

There is as much debate today about the diagnosis—the explanation—of family disruption as there is about its possible cure. And this is understandable. If our prescriptions for addressing family problems fail to understand the real causes, they will rise dramatically like a Fourth of July rocket but soon sputter in the wind and crash to the ground. Solutions must fit the conditions producing the difficulties families face. But to determine the true causes is not a simple matter. It is one thing to overwhelm the reader with depressing facts about family deterioration, as we probably did in the last chapter. It is another thing to advance coherent explanations that truly orient us to what realistically can be done to ameliorate the individual and social costs of family troubles.

Popular discourse proposes, often quite dogmatically, several explanations. "The breakdown of morals" is a frequently heard explanation. Then there is the related view that family problems are due to modern "selfishness" and "materialism." Some people blame the advent of the cinema, the automobile (those suggestive and unsupervised back seats), "the pill," TV, or now the internet (sexual chat rooms, on-line dating, pornography). Some people blame feminism or the fact that women are now working in the wage economy. These views deserve serious consideration.

But many of us want to refine such explanations and place them within larger contexts of analysis and meaning. Appeals to our newborn selfishness assume that once we were virtuous and then suddenly lost our moral character. This seems like an act of self-congratulation by those who remember when there were fewer divorces and nonmarital births. Being the anxious creatures we are, we humans are a fairly self-seeking lot, although our self-interest is often mixed with surprising amounts of empathy and care.[37] But were people fifty years ago really more virtuous across the board, or did they simply work out their human fallibilities in different ways? Furthermore, although new inventions such as the pill, cars, movies, TV, and the internet have changed behavior, aren't they part of something larger— some deeper trends that undergird them all? We think that there are deeper trends.

Three Causes: Three Cures

We nominate three clusters of causes—cultural, social systemic, and psychological—to account for the contemporary struggles of families. The order is important. The cultural causes are listed first because we think that they constitute the major forces bringing about present-day family changes. The social systemic and psychological factors are moved significantly, although not totally, by cultural trends. But these causal forces are interactional; social and psychological forces rebound back on culture and further amplify their consequences. The social systemic and psychological causes add features that are not necessarily implicit in the cultural trajectories as such.

Since we give the highest priority to the cultural shifts fueling family disruption, it will be no surprise to see us emphasize the importance of cultural visions, values, and goals as major sources of a cure. This is why we have emphasized the reaffirmation of religious and cultural traditions. As they have functioned in the past, these traditions likely will be our major source for the values, norms, and sensibilities guiding families in the future. This may be true even if these traditions are appropriated in more symbolic and less literal ways in the future. But, as should be clear to the reader by now: *the two of us are not just unreconstructed traditionalists.* We seek to understand and affirm traditions as first steps toward their appropriate reconstruction on selected aspects of their family theories. Although shifts in cultural values are the main cause of family decline and reconfigured cultural values the main source for cure, social system patterns and psychological stress are important as well. Solutions must address these factors as well.

Culture: The Rise of Individualism

The major cultural trend affecting the American family is the rise of individualism. Individualism springs from a deep cultural vision. It was shaped in part by the future oriented view of life found in Judaism and Christianity, the major religions shaping Western and American culture, at least until recent years. But modern individualism also contained new emphases on the values of reason, individual autonomy, and skepticism about tradition—themes developed in different ways in the Enlightenment philosophies of David Hume, John Locke, and Immanuel Kant. Nearly every recent historian who has written extensively on the family has emphasized the role of the culture of individualism that entered modern consciousness during the eighteenth and nineteenth centuries. Historians Edward Shorter and Lawrence Stone have written about the role played by cultural individualism in unsettling families.[38] Some writers believe this new individualism left us rootless and normless in our everyday behavior. Others believe it replaced an old tradition-saturated ethic with a new one, different in content but just as coherent. Shorter belongs to this latter school when he writes: "The content of these modern values is very different, sanctioning individualism over community allegiance and self-realization over collective solidarity. But the players are all clear about the rules and adhere to them." This new individualistic culture put fresh emphasis on romantic love, personalized mate selection, sexual satisfaction as an end in itself, and it gave less control to parents, extended family, and community.

But it would be wrong to emphasize individualism without mentioning again the associated rise of technical rationality as a cultural value. Max Weber opened our eyes to this new cultural value, as we mentioned above. But the appreciation of technical reason should be seen first as a new value springing from a deep cultural vision with several sources—the Protestant work ethic, Enlightenment individualism, and the new empirical sciences. Individualism and technical rationality were brothers in arms; they were both motivated by a deeper desire to control the future for the enhancement of personal satisfactions.

Some might say, "See, I told you so. It is really selfishness and the breakdown of our moral values that have brought about family disruption." Yes and no. It would be wrong to believe that in traditional societies built around obedience to kin, church, and patriarch that people did not find ways to be self-seeking, controlling, and seditious. It is also true that higher degrees of individual initiative and autonomy do not necessarily lead to more raw selfishness; it may be possible to organize heightened autonomy into a variety of responsible ethical systems. Indeed, we believe that can happen in a well lived ethic of equal regard of the kind that we propose. Nonetheless, it is safe to say that modern individualism has interacted with other forces in ways that have been hard on families. And some social observers think that these individualistic cultural forces are so deep, so ingrained in the fabric of our cultural and institutional life, that there is no way to derail their negative consequences for families. The formula goes like this: the more individualism, the less family solidarity. Hence, we are told to face reality, learn to live with weaker families, and do the best that we can.[39] We should lower our expectations, be satisfied with picking up the pieces, and remain content to simply lessen the pain. In fact, from the perspective of these social determinists, all efforts to change these trends are expressions of either cultural coercion or idle whistling in the wind—either authoritarianism or mere wishful thinking.

In connection with culture, we must mention two other realities—patriarchy and racism. They both must be defined as cultural values. As cultural values, they interact with Western individualism and produce a wide range of strange and devastating results. Patriarchy is the cultural attitude that says men are more rational, more authoritative, and therefore should have both the privilege and honor of guiding large portions of society. Racism is the cultural attitude that says that some groups are more intelligent, competent, and trustworthy than others and therefore should have more privileges. Racism ends in discrimination against certain groups—discrimination that invariably hurts them and weakens their families. Both patriarchy and racism are in decline, but both are still with us. The ethic of equal regard championed in this book is designed to address both—lingering patriarchy in gender relations and the remaining racism in group relations.

The central example of racism in the U.S. has been the discrimination of whites against blacks that began in the use of slaves by the early American settlers. The recognition of the devastation of slavery for the entire history of African American families has been a subject of considerable research and debate. We agree with recent new turns in this scholarship put forth by Harvard sociologist Orlando Patterson in his *Rituals of Blood* (1998)—slavery and its aftermath had tragic consequences for black families, men, women, gender relations, and children—even worse than we used to think. Justice requires that this be recognized and that a variety of efforts be instituted to give wise and special help to black families. In short, the cultural values of individualism, patriarchy, and racism interact to harm families. They also combine in various ways with social system trends to further harm families, a topic we turn to next.

Culture and Social System:
Market Family versus State Family

The most powerful explanation of family tensions comes from observing how cultural individualism and modern social systems interact. When cultural individualism interacts with technical reason, it is actually interacting with two huge social systemic embodiments of it, i.e., the market on one hand and modern governmental bureaucracies on the other. Technical reason is not simply something in our minds—a mode of thinking. We put technical reason to work in our social systems. Both Jürgen Habermas and Alan Wolfe write about one kind of technical rationality that expresses itself in the cost-benefit logics of the market and another kind of technical rationality that expresses itself in the service bureaucracies of modern industrial states.[40] On the one hand, the efficiency and profit demands of the market more and more suck all families—both fathers and mothers and even the children—into the cost-benefit thinking of this sector of modern society. On the other hand, bureaucratic efficiency spreads into our lives, quietly robs us of our initiatives, and makes families passive and dependent clients of well-meaning but controlling governmental agencies. Both of these expressions of technical rationality have potential harmful effects on families.

Market Family

Sociologist Alan Wolfe (1989) says that technical rationality expressed in the market produced what he calls the "market family." This is the family increasingly absorbed into the needs of modern capitalism, which more and more thinks of human and family relationships in analogy to profits, losses, and the exchange value of commodities. Wolfe thinks the neoclassical economic theory and its application to the understanding of the family in the writings of Gary Becker and Richard Posner are great rationalizations of the market family. The hope of the market family—and the ideologies that feed it—is that its sheer affluence will soften the blow of the forces of disintegration that are pulling it apart. It is true: with affluence the pain may lessen, but if we can trust the insights of clinicians such as Judith Wallerstein (1989) and researchers such as McLanahan and Sandefur, the damage done by family disruption, no matter how much it is cushioned by wealth, may linger for years and into succeeding generations. Demographer Ron Lesthaege examines large chunks of Western demographic data and concludes that family disruption in fact paralleled the increase in affluence that occurred at the end of the nineteenth century and, again, during the 1960s and early 1970s. [41] These were the periods in which cultural individualism produced by the Enlightenment was exacerbated by the additional cost-benefit mentality of the spreading market—thus producing the context for the emerging market family. The pill, the car, movies, and TV are not just lucky inventions but some of the many expressions of spreading technical rationality further stimulated by market dynamics.

Both Marxists and rational choice economists, in their different ways, have argued that changing patterns of economic life have greatly affected the shape of families. The move by large numbers of men in the nineteenth century from the farm to the wage economy of town and city created the contours of the industrial or Victorian family. This created the so-called traditional family consisting of the wage earning husband and domestic mother, a pattern that actually put new economic power in the hands of husbands and made wives and mothers both more dependent on husbands and more confined to the domestic realm. This move placed families—especially men—into the rhythms of market pressures. Nineteenth century historians are full of stories about harried, competitive, profit-driven husbands and their restricted wives. These largely domestic women often used their pent-up energies to lead their husbands and sons to the mass evangelistic meetings of the Second Great Awakening; they wanted to save the souls of the men in their lives— not only from sin but from the emerging logics of modernity and the competitive market.[42] Marxists, of course, see this new middle-class family as the bourgeois or Victorian family and believe it was bad—indeed, very bad. Men and women, they think, did not really love each other in these families; there was too much economic dependency by women and too much economic domination of men for real "sex love," to use Engels's term, to occur.[43] On the other hand, rational choice economists view these nineteenth century moves into the wage economy as a step toward expanding economic choice and more efficient satisfactions of our basic interests. They also believe that this step by families toward the market was completed in the twentieth century when women also entered the wage economy, thereby bringing both husband and wife, father and mother, into the benefits, logics, and constraints of an increasingly fast-paced world of business and industry.[44]

Liberal feminists have characterized this last step as a matter of liberation. To cope with modernization is, for them, to *join* it and directly gain the benefits earlier enjoyed only by men.[45] Cultural conservatives, on the other hand, have viewed women's step into the wage economy as the final capitulation to modernity; their strategy for coping with it was to be *halfway in and halfway out.* They preached that men were supposed to be on the inside of the modernizing process and women were to slow this same process down, humanize it, and contain it, primarily from outside—from the vantage point of the private and protected home. *It is not clear that either of these strategies is satisfactory. This is why, in this book, we will support a strategy whereby both men and women can in principle be both inside and outside the market. Our strategy gives both men and women access to the market, lowers the time they invest in their jobs, liberates them both to have more time for child care and domestic duties, and takes steps to limit the influence of the market on the life-space of the home.* This approach can be implemented in a variety of ways but most specifically by our recommendation to create a paid work week of no more than a total of sixty hours for couples with young children. We will develop that proposal in chapter 7.

The creation of the market family has put pressure on all parents who are unprepared to cope with the increasing technological character of modern employment. Racism is part of the explanation for the disappearance of jobs from the inner cites where most minorities actually reside. But technology and the need of business for highly trained workers is another reason for this disappearance. For example, these two together—racism and the needs of a technological society—have conspired to deprive inner-city blacks of desperately needed economic opportunities, an issue that Harvard sociologist William Julius Wilson has investigated in detail in his *The Truly Disadvantaged* (1987) and *When Work Disappears* (1996). The lack of jobs for African American men is clearly one of the dominant reasons, among many, why marriages have declined and nonmarital births have increased in the black community. The computer revolution exacerbates this trend toward joblessness. It creates what some have called the "digital divide"—the wall separating those who have been trained to run sophisticated computers and those who have not. Those who don't have these skills get left behind, remain poor, and have enormous difficulties supporting families and tending to their children.

State Family

The state family, of course, can be equally fragile. Governments can subtly and silently take over family functions rather than helping families to help themselves. We contend, as will be argued below, that modern states have a vital role to play in supporting families but not if they go so far as to undermine what families can normally do better for themselves than any other agency. This is what Alan Wolfe (1989) and David Popenoe (1988) think is happening in the well-funded and expansive welfare programs of the Nordic countries. This is why the indices of family breakdown in the U.S. and Sweden are roughly similar, even though the former is the great example of the market family and the latter of the state family.

But the capacity of government programs to undercut families can happen in the U.S. as well. As Dizard and Gadlin argue, the interaction of individualism and capitalism requires a strong state to support those who get ground up in this dynamism and thereby fall through the cracks. But it is also possible to get trapped in the welfare system— to become dependent upon it and allow these dependencies to take the place of spouse, marriage, extended family, and immediate community. Even political liberals such as David Ellwood and Mary Jo Bane confessed in their *Welfare Realities* (1994) that this had been allowed to happen in the welfare programs preceding the 1996 reforms. Although they would not have solved the dependency producing dynamics of welfare by going toward devolution, their book is a convincing testimony, written by pro-welfare scholars, of how the so-called state family can be created by well-intentioned bureaucracies. In countries like the U.S., the stresses of the market family are the lot of those who succeed in the wage economy, while the dependencies of the state family are the destiny of those who do not succeed in the market. Increasingly, families are getting whiplashed with a double motion—the technical rationality of the market that forces on them its cost-benefit calculations, and the technical rationality of state bureaucracies that creates a logic of family dependency on government. Solutions must work to curb and balance both of these expressions of uninhibited technical rationality.

Psychological Causes

Modern families are under tremendous psychological stress. It is not simply because many people have been raised by inadequate, neglectful, or even abusive parents. There are doubtless many inadequate parents and multitudes of poorly prepared husbands and wives making a mess of relating to one another. But the psychological aspects of family problems go deeper than the emotional problems of individuals functioning destructively in relationships with their spouses, children, and other relatives. Individualism, technical rationality, and their expressions in the modernizing forces of market and government function to weaken ties of nuclear family with extended family, lower dependencies of husbands and wives, leave less time for parents to spend with their children, throw children prematurely into the powerful influences of the market and market-fed popular culture, and leave the young too much under the influence of peers and media without the supervision of adults.

All of these influences produce increased psychological stress. It can take a million forms. Freud saw family problems as primarily a result of Oedipal conflicts—an overdetermined superego that leaves young adults (primarily men) with rigid, neurotic, and maladaptive consciences. But Freud was blind to the problem of modernization behind these observations, i.e., the fact that the individualism and autonomy required by modernization by definition place children in conflict with the traditions of their fathers and, of course, their mothers. Hence, psychoanalysis, as are most of the modern psychotherapies, was a pro-modernizing cultural vehicle.[46] To solve conflicts between sons and fathers by weakening the superego and strengthening the ego is to vote on the side of modernization and against tradition.

The two of us believe that this conflict needs to be mediated, but not necessarily by taking sides, i.e., modernity over tradition *or* tradition vanquishing modernity. For the most part, the modern psychotherapies threw their weight on the side of the pro-modernizing cultural and social systemic forces of the twentieth century. Freud certainly did, and this was his psychological way of addressing family problems. On the other hand, sociologist Nancy Chodorow (1989) and psychotherapist Jessica Benjamin (1988) are more sensitive than Freud about how modernization interacts with the psychological development of the individual. Speaking to these issues more from a feminist perspective, they see family problems rooted in the strong differentiation during the nineteenth century between the public spheres of men and the private-domestic spheres of women—a process that throws a shadow over our lives even today. This means that mothers primarily raise young boys in the first years of their lives. As a consequence, the little boy first identifies with the mother but must later tear himself away from—actually re-press—this warm, affectionate, and sensuous relation with the mother in order to identify with the father in the manly disciplines of the market-driven world of public life. This leaves men with a compensating hyper-masculinity that makes them unsuited to relate to the intimacy of child care and intersubjective life of husband and wife needed so des-perately for the modern family.

For Chodorow and Benjamin, this is the source of many of the problems that grip family life today. What is, for them, the cure? They propose instituting a more reciprocal rela-tion between public and private spheres so the fathers are part of childrearing and mothers more a part of the public sphere—from the very beginning of both marriage and the birth of offspring. Hence, the social space between these two spheres of life should be intentionally reduced and the mod-ernization process guided and restrained to fit the human scale of things.

This kind of cure addresses psychological strains by re-forming both the culture and the social system. The culture must change. Men must learn to value domestic responsibili-ties—especially child care. And women should learn to value involvement in community and public life. And both of these things should happen without allowing the market and the wage economy to take over all of our lives, either the lives of men and fathers or women and mothers. But the social system must change as well. A huge number of adjust-ments must occur in the workplace, in child care, in the re-lations between work and home. We will discuss many of these necessary work-family adjustments in later chapters.

But there are other psychological solutions that start more immediately with individual family members and less at the grand scale of culture and social system. Many of these initiatives are educational in character; some have to do with counseling and psychotherapy. According to the educational and counseling view, the huge cultural trend toward individualism and the vast social systemic shifts fired by technical reason can be creatively guided and recontextualized. Their negative consequences can be more self-consciously guided and contained by good education and therapy. There are quite remarkable new breakthroughs in premarital and marital education, in the scientific analysis of marital communication, in understanding child development, and in organizing and strengthening communities to prepare for and support good marriages and healthy families. Many of these new approaches are useful for couples throughout the life cycle. Even though most of these programs do not directly address the macro-cultural and social system changes that have put so much pressure on marriage and family, they implicitly help us cope with these forces anyway.

The Three Directions

To date and court, to marry, stay married, be reasonably happy, and raise children successfully, couples will need several things. They will require high degrees of commitment, high levels of communicative skills, sufficient financial resources, sufficient time for family tasks and enjoyments, and community supports. Commitment is the result of a cultural vision about the importance of marriage. Communicative skills come first from our families of origin but can be refined by intentional education. But we must have them both—commitment *and* skills—because marriages have fewer external supports. Having enough time for family responsibilities must come from a new cultural commitment to attain it and a new will to force our various social systems to provide for it. Having sufficient financial resources for families must come from a combination of circumstances derived from our cultural view of work and from the effectiveness of the social systems of market and government. The need for wider community supports of a nongovernmental kind raises issues about the role of the nongovernmental institutions of civil society.

Hence, throughout the following pages, we will be working at three levels of human action—culture, social systems, and individual persons. Our society must learn to think at several different levels if it wants to address family issues. We wish it were not so complicated, but it is. Our society is torn by conflicts over the family because the different parties to the debate come with different diagnoses emphasizing one or another of these frameworks. They offer different solutions that follow from their diagnosis. Some want to change the culture. Some want to change the workplace, taxation, and welfare. Some want to change persons through marriage education and counseling.

We say keep all three of them in mind; progress on family issues involves a balance among them. Our cultural visions can be reformulated and improved; our social systems can be fine-tuned; our psychological and communicative skills can be strengthened. All of this will make us more genuinely bilingual and bicultural—more able to deeply cherish, preserve, and reconstruct our various cultural heritages and do so in ways that help us live and cope with the forces of modernization.

5

Culture: Marriage as Public Philosophy and Policy?

"Marriage is a personal relationship between two people. The state should have nothing to do with it." How many times have you heard such remarks? Or this: "Marriage is a relationship between a couple and their God. It is primarily a matter for church and synagogue." Both of these sentiments, widely heard in coffee shops and read in newspapers when Louisiana in 1997 passed its covenant marriage law, are prevalent in the public consciousness. Some individuals objected when that state created, in addition to its regular no-fault marriage, another alternative called "covenant marriage" with higher standards for both entrance and exit. Many people criticized the move even though this new marriage option was not required and could be freely chosen by couples. Many religious congregations objected as well. Some ministers and priests held that marriage is a matter for religious institutions—not the state.

The public knows that a couple must obtain a license in order for a marriage to be valid, but many people are not sure why. It is commonly known that when ministers or rabbis officiate at weddings, they represent the state as well as their religious denominations. Yet many people see the license as an irritation. "It is just a piece of paper," we are told. It does not get to the heart of what makes a genuine marriage. And the idea of a "covenant marriage" upheld by the state—what is the meaning of that?

When we hear of other ways in which the state is involved in marriage, it makes many of us all the more nervous. Certainly at the time of divorce the state is there, often in heavy-handed and clumsy ways. Then there are taxes: some couples actually pay more to Uncle Sam when they get married. Some people call it a "marriage penalty." But many experts doubt whether there really is a tax disadvantage for certain groups of married couples. If there is such a penalty, does it discourage marriage? Furthermore, should it be corrected? This means, in effect, should the state remedy laws that may discourage marriage—laws that it helped create in the first place? And finally, how far should the state use its power to actually encourage and reward marriage?

Some people are perplexed to learn that between 1998 and 2000, the governors of Florida, Arkansas, Arizona, New Mexico, Oklahoma, Utah, and Wisconsin took steps to lower the divorce rate, encourage marriage, and educate citizens about the value of marriage. And, of course, the most stunning recent example of federal government involvement in marriage was the 1996 federal welfare reforms. They came about, in good measure, because the older system called Aid to Families with Dependent Children (AFDC) was thought to discourage marriage among recipients. The new system, it was hoped, would encourage marriage and the two-parent family and discourage nonmarital births.

We could go on and on with such examples. But the basic question is this: to what extent should marriage be an interest of the state? This is an issue that this book must confront. We already have said that the renewal and reconstruction of marriage is a central strategy for fostering a sound family life in the U.S. We also acknowledged that marriage has been in various ways an important value of the major religious traditions. Indeed, they have been the leading carriers of the customs, ceremonies, and meanings that have surrounded the institution of marriage. Bring Protestants, Roman Catholics, Orthodox, Jews, Muslims, and Neo-Confucians more deeply into American public life and, in spite of their increasing secularization and modernization, marriage will emerge as a central value.

But in all modern nations, marriage is to some degree an interest of the state as well. Why is this so? Should it be? Furthermore, should religious traditions have the right to influence government on these matters? Finally, does the government have an interest in marriage independently of what religious traditions might have to say on the matter? We believe that the state should be interested in marriage as a part of its family policies. There are certain things it can do to make marriage accountable, encourage marriage, strengthen it, and help it flourish. *But the state should offer its supports and encouragements within a broader public philosophy that orchestrates its specific contributions with those of other sectors of society.* In the end, both state and civil society (including religions) should be interested in supporting marriage, but for reasons that should be distinguished, not necessarily separated.

In recent hisory, the state has primarily viewed marriage as a public health issue. For religion and the cultural sensibilities it creates, marriage is primarily a matter of commitment—a way of living out a divine command, the dynamics of the divine life, or some fundamental principle of the universe. For most religions, the functional goods that marriage creates are important but secondary. Religious institutions inject various "intrinsic moments" into marriage that resist reducing it to its functional goods. By intrinsic moment, we mean certain values and moral claims that are ends in themselves and not primarily means or instruments of material and psychological satisfaction. As the state must respect other aspects of our cultural heritages, it should respect these intrinsic moments carried by many religions and do nothing to directly undermine the larger cultural, and religiocultural, meanings associated with this institution. Various aspects of society should cooperate in enhancing and protecting both the intrinsic and functional goods of marriage.

Marriage and Public Health

Marriage is increasingly being viewed as a public health issue. Strong economic reasons for the goods of marriage can be advanced by the neoclassical economic theories of Gary Becker and Richard Posner—reasons mainly dealing with the efficiencies that marriage produces and the rather wide range of human interests that it satisfies. We already have referred to the social science research summarized by Professor Linda Waite about the multiple health benefits of marriage—more mental and physical health, longer lives, more satisfying sex, and more wealth. At the 1998 annual conference of the Coalition for Marriage, Family, and Couples Education, Judge James Sheridan from Adrian, Michigan, distributed the graphs and figures from Waite's article to his audience. He did this to explain and support the concept of the Community Marriage Policy that he had helped establish in Adrian. This was a policy that organized ministers, justices of the peace, medical doctors, social workers, teachers, and marriage counselors to support a community-wide policy promoting longer waiting periods, the use of premarital inventories, and marriage education for all couples planning to get married in the community. Judge Sheridan was emphatic in repeatedly saying:

Marriage is not just a religious matter. Nor is it simply a private affair. Marriage is a matter of the public good—a concern of the law and the state. Bad marriages cost me money. They increase my tax bill. They make the streets I walk less safe. The kids from bad marriages run wild, get in trouble, have car accidents, and go to jail. Paying for jail increases my taxes.

Judge Sheridan's message was effective, at least in Adrian. The appeal to public health, public safety, and lower taxes cleared the space for the acceptance of marriage as a public issue—as a matter of public policy. But actually, his argument went beyond public policy as such. It raised wider issues pertaining to public philosophy. What he was calling for had very few, if any, direct implications for either law or government action as such. Judge Sheridan was calling for cooperation among different sectors of that community —among ministers, rabbis, justices of the peace, marriage counselors and educators, and other professionals relevant to the institution of marriage. He was asking for a cultural transformation—a new "marriage culture" that would replace the emerging "culture of divorce" and the "culture of nonmarriage." This new marriage culture would not force or pressure people to get married. In fact, it might sometimes discourage specific couples who were neither ready nor suited for each other. Its goal would be to help people get married well and prepare for it carefully and intentionally. Judge Sheridan was creating a public philosophy for marriage that would encompass more specific public policies that might eventuate from it.

Judge Sheridan may have been given to a bit of overstatement. The program he was describing and advocating did not remove marriages from religion; it extended marriage as a matter of legitimate interest to several spheres of society all cooperating together. His explicit language, however, does signal a new phenomonon in our society, i.e., *the increasing tendency to justify marriage in the name of public health—the same way we justify the public regulation of water and electricity companies or the same way we do paving and maintaining our city streets.* These things are good for both the individual and collective health. His language appeared to take marriage away from its religious justification in divine ordinance, covenant, and sacrament and place it into the realm of public contract for the purposes of public health.

The Reformation and Marriage as an Interest of the State

From another angle of vision, however, Judge Sheridan is not as radical as he first appears. He was not doing something completely new, even though the precedents for his actions largely have been forgotten. He was, at least in part, doing something quite old and very classical; it goes back, at least for Western societies, to the time of the Protestant Reformation. To understand how marriage became a matter of state interest yet also supported by a variety of interlocking and cooperative spheres of society, we must return to sixteenth century Germany. This will help us understand the origins of the broader public philosophy undergirding the mutual relation between state, law, and religion in the West's customary widespread, multidimensional, cultural support for marriage. This cooperative relation between the various spheres of society on matters affecting marriage was an ideal that Judge Sheridan was implicitly suggesting should be dusted off, taken from the shelf, and implemented once again—with some very intentional cultural muscle.

The Reformation was complex. It not only gave birth to Protestantism and a new understanding of the status of the individual conscience, it brought about a new alignment between religion and the state that had profound implications for the status of marriage. It is this realignment that is our main interest here. It was the Reformation that made marriage first of all a secular affair subject to state registration, witness, sanction, and regulation for all citizens. Only after this occurred was marriage a matter of ecclesial blessing. This shift made marriage more than just a private and ecclesial affair; it made marriage a matter of public concern and an issue of the social or common good. Marriage became a "social estate."[47]

Before the Reformation, marriage in Western nations was administered primarily by the Roman Catholic Church. For centuries, marriage had been mainly an ecclesial affair— generally officiated by the priest, often done in the church, and requiring church recognition for its validity. Even then, however, its validity before the church did not *depend completely* on the presence of a priest or even the presence of witnesses. The dominant view held that the only thing absolutely required to establish a valid marriage was for a duly baptized man and woman to say in the present tense that "I take you to be my wife" or "I take you to be my husband."[48] Marriage could not be coerced; it had to be freely chosen. But it did not absolutely require either a priest or a witness to be considered valid by the church.

These were the stipulations of Roman Catholic canon law, a synthesis between Roman Catholic theology and elements of both Roman and German civil law. Many scholars consider the accomplishments of Catholic canon law to have established what legal scholar John Witte calls the "genetic code" of Western marriage and family theory. Marriage was a matter of free decision by the couple involved. A father could no longer legally give his daughter for marriage against her will. A young man and woman could, in principle, no longer be used against their wills as tools of family ambitions and political alliances. But marriage could be, and often was, primarily a private affair that was only secondarily made valid by the church on the basis of the testimony of the couple.

Like so many great cultural accomplishments, the consequences of Catholic canon law were ambiguous. On the positive side, the role of consent in marriage was elevated. Because this required the consent of the bride as well as the groom, the status of women was advanced. Polygyny was firmly outlawed in European countries where the church's canon law ruled, thereby breaking down the privilege of powerful and wealthy men to hoard marriageable women while poor men remained unmarried and generally childless. This, as historian David Herlihy (1985) has argued, gradually led to a democratization of marriage, making it more widely available to women, and especially to men, of common means.

On the negative side, it led to a social practice that is not widely remembered by contemporary society—the phenomenon of "secret" or "clandestine" marriage. Since a marriage, to be valid, only required a man and a woman to say "I do" in the present tense—without witnesses, without a priest, and without the registration and certification of the state—many couples suddenly would emerge claiming to be married. Or, after a pregnancy, the couple would claim that they had once said "yes, I do" in each other's presence. But it often became more complicated. After the pregnancy, one member might claim that they both said "I take you" to be my husband or wife, but the other partner might deny that such words had ever been spoken. Then there were cases when an ambitious man or woman, wishing to marry into a wealthy and powerful family, would claim that the two of them had once consented to marry and that therefore he or she was entitled to the status of a son or daughter-in-law and, incidentally, a rightful share of the inheritance. And then there were cases in which valid consent did occur, but one or other party would later deny it in order to escape from the marriage.[49] Hence, the same steps that had increased the autonomy of the couple, elevated the status of women, and removed marriage from the arbitrary control of parents and extended family had also led in some instances to higher degrees of confusion, duplicity, manipulation, and betrayal.

Although Luther made many negative remarks about Roman Catholic canon law, much of it was adopted by the legal scholars of the Reformation, amended in selected ways, and used as the foundation of marriage and family codes in modern states influenced by Protestantism. One of these amendments introduced a startling and contentious new idea. *It made marriage a civil affair requiring registration with the state and the publishing of banns so that the community would know about the impending wedding.* This made it possible to bring to public light any impediments such as bigamy, polygyny, incest, or other irregularities that could invalidate the marriage. Marriage still retained for the Reformers a religious meaning. Although it was no longer seen as a sacrament and in itself part of the drama of salvation, as it had been for the Roman Catholic Church, it was still viewed as holy and ordained by God in creation for the good of humankind. Marriage was understood as guiding and ordering human sexuality, increasing the comfort and mutual assistance of husband and wife, and for the procreation of children and their education in responsible spiritual, moral, and political virtues. For these reasons, it was commonly thought that marriages also should be blessed by the church before parents, witnesses, and the wider worshiping community.

The move to make marriage a public institution accountable to the wider community gradually reduced the number of clandestine marriages and the turmoil they injected into the social fabric. This was the beginning of the systematic involvement of the modern state in marriage. This established the cooperative relation between religion and the state in creating the meaning and order of marriage. True, much of the meaning of marriage was still supplied by religion, but the state helped give the institution public accountability and status. The emergence of the modern state with its firm boundaries, clearer lines of authority, and more coherent legal and legislative procedures also helped consolidate the process. Soon Geneva, England, and Scotland followed in giving varying degrees of control over marriage to the state. The Catholic Church itself, although reluctant to move into a partnership with the state on marriage, did take vigorous steps at the Council of Trent (1545–1563) to make marriage more accountable, at least to the religious community. Its Decree Tametsi (1563) required marriages to be registered with the church and contracted before a priest. It mandated the publishing of banns and the postponement of cohabitation until after the wedding.

As the modern state developed in Roman Catholic areas, governments required the public registration of marriage in those countries as well. The Protestant amendments to canon law influenced countries such as Holland and Scotland. These amendments were extremely influential on the view of marriage as a support of the commonwealth found in seventeenth and eighteenth England. This same legal tradition influenced the Northeastern colonies of the

United States. More Roman Catholic versions of the canon law tradition influenced law in France, Italy, Spain, Central and South America, as well as Florida, Louisiana, Arizona, New Mexico, and California in the U.S.

It would be wrong to suggest that governments had never been concerned with the regulation of marriage before the Reformation. There were Athenian and Roman legal traditions addressing marriage, but these generally applied only to free individuals and not to the lower classes and certainly not to slaves. German and Frankish tribes and clans had their legal traditions, often unevenly applied as the fortunes of the kings and territories that they ruled waxed and waned. Roman Catholic canon law brought order and universality about marriage and family into the European territories, but it did this for centuries more or less independently of civil authorities.

Religious Pluralism and the Need to Appreciate Past Accomplishments

Protestants and Catholics have many differences in their views of marriage, but behind these are even deeper commonalities due to their shared use of the canon law tradition. These are the sources that give the two authors of this book, in spite of their Protestant and Catholic differences, a deeper shared history that is nearly forgotten but that still functions at the level of implicit legal and cultural codes. Of course, both Protestantism and Catholicism depended heavily on the Jewish scriptures, especially Genesis I and II and the great analogy found in the book of Hosea between God's faithfulness to Israel and the loyalty required between husband and wife. These Jewish sources greatly influenced the view of marriage found in Islam as well. As we have suggested above, there is a sense in which the massive traditions of Judaism, Islam, Catholicism, and Protestantism all have deep roots in the marital vision of ancient Israel. All of them are fed by the Abrahamic religious and legal tradition. There are deeply shared religiocultural traditions about the meaning of marriage among these otherwise distinct American religious groups.

But it was the Reformation that established the idea that marriage is a social estate for the common good and that the state, as differentiated from religious institutions, has a crucial role in its public ordering. This revolution created most decisively the state's involvement with marriage and the collaborative relation between government and other sectors of society for its defense and enhancement. This is the model that has influenced much of the Western marriage tradition, including that of the United States.

This is the heritage to which various newer groups in American life should relate. This is the legacy that we should respect as we deliberate about how to evolve toward a more inclusive future. As new traditions move into American life—Islamic, various Asian traditions, and even secularism as a tradition—it would be foolish for us to fail to recognize the wisdom of this inherited collaborative relation between state and religiocultural traditions. Against the background of the increasing deinstitutionalization and privatization of marriage, the rise of nonmarital births, informal family formation, rapid and costly marriage and family dissolution, and serial marriage, *we should think twice before pursuing a course of action that accelerates the declining public status of marriage and family formation*. It is not extreme to think that we may be returning to the confusions of secret or clandestine marriage of an earlier era or, perhaps, developing our own form of these essentially private arrangements today. The processes of modernization, as we indicated above, are probably most responsible for this privatization process. It is true: some people see this as a cultural advance—a great new step toward increased liberty and sexual freedom. In contrast to this view, we believe that retaining a view of marriage as public and seeing it as the central institution for the organization of human sexuality and procreation will be crucial for preserving and enhancing the flourishing of families and the children they give birth to and nourish.

The meaning of marital commitment has been carried principally by religious institutions. This may be true in the future but with a wider range of religious traditions playing a role in the total cultural process. *We have not in the past turned to the state for the development of this commitment nor for the visions and symbols that give marriage its meaning, but we have turned to the state for public accountability and practical support.* And in the new pluralism that is emerging, we should affirm the accomplishments of the past as we strive for a more inclusive future.

The New Pluralism and the Need for a Double Language

One reason that state and religion in the past have cooperated on marriage is because there have been resources for a double language. Even when the language of religion reigned supreme, there was often a second and subordinate language that assisted with the economic, legal, and biological aspects of marriage and family life. Indeed, there was often a distinctively religious language. For Judaism, Protestantism, and Catholicism, this language was created by the founding stories of the Jewish tradition—the creation of Adam and Eve as male and female (Gen. 1:27), their reflection of the image of God (Gen. 1:27), God's charge to them to be fruitful (Gen. 1:28), and the joint dominion and stewardship of male and female over creation (Gen. 1:28). It is in these texts that we learn "it is not good" for a human to be alone (Gen. 2:18) and therefore a man "leaves his father and mother and clings to his wife, and they become one flesh" (Gen. 2:24). From the standpoint of these religions, these scriptures have the weight of divine revelation, and this is entirely appropriate. From this perspective, Judaism and Christianity have received the same revelation and been informed by the same divine commandments.

But what weight should such scriptures have in a public philosophy for marriage and family, especially one that might also influence the concrete details of public policy in law and legislation? Clearly, they cannot have the weight of revelation. And they cannot have binding power as such over the wider public and those traditions, religious or secular, that do not draw on these scriptures.

They can have, however, the power of what Hans-Georg Gadamer (1982) has called "the classical." By the idea of the classical, he meant something more than an interesting piece of literature or art and more than the aesthetic style of a particular historical period. He meant a document or monument that has become central to the formation of cultural consciousness. It is classical because "through the constant proving of itself, [it] sets before us something that is true." It has had defining power, been tested over the centuries, proven compelling time and again, and continues to influence us unconsciously even if we largely have forgotten, neglected, or rejected it. The dominant Western marriage traditions have several such classics—Genesis, Hosea, certain teachings of Jesus and Paul, the writings of Aristotle, the canon law, etc. These classics give us several things— general visions of life, the general place within it of marriage and family, indices of the goods of marriage and family, statements about the sacred dignity of men and women, affirmations of the intrinsic good of children, and certain principles governing the formation and dissolution of marriage. It is these classics, and others we could mention, that have shaped the Western tradition of marriage and family, at least up until recent decades.

Some of these classics have had the power to persuade and convince because they contained a double language—a *naturalistic and philosophical* language that conceptualized certain regularities of human nature as well as a *language of symbol, metaphor, and narrative* that surrounded this natural and philosophical language and thereby gave it a wider religious meaning. In the West, much of the philosophical and naturalistic language that went into the formation of Western family theory came from Greek philosophy, mainly the writings of Aristotle. It was Aristotle who first developed the ideas that the family was the basic unit of society, preceding in time and function the formation of the state. Aristotle believed that both men and women have a deep desire to "leave behind them an image of themselves"—hence, a desire to have children. He taught that the family is also a place for the mutual comfort and assistance of husband and wife—"an association established by nature for the supply of men's everyday wants." These affirmations were all stated in the tones of philosophy and Greek styles of biopsychology. His views were expressed in language analogous to the contemporary languages of health, economics, and evolutionary psychology—languages within which so much of the modern debate about marriage and family proceeds. This is a different language altogether than the language of Genesis, so crucial for the traditions of Judaism, Islam, and Christianity. In these religions, marriage and family are established first of all through the language of faith and divine command.

But, in reality, the development of the Western marriage and family tradition was a matter of bringing these two languages together. There were other languages brought into the mix as well—for instance, the language of secular law. Catholic canon law built on the language of scripture and Greek philosophy. But it also built on the foundations of Roman and, to some extent, German law. These were technical languages governing issues of inheritance, contract, consent, degrees of consanguinity, and the grounds of marital dissolution.

Medieval Roman Catholic theology, especially the writings of Thomas Aquinas, brought the three languages—the language of the Bible, the language of Greek philosophy (Aristotle and the Stoics), and the language of Roman and German law—together in a remarkably sophisticated way. This created a differentiated language with which to speak of marriage and family matters. In Aquinas, at the highest and most general level, there was the religious language of symbol, metaphor, and narrative. This was the language used to speak about marriage as a sacrament—the central value of Roman Catholic theology of marriage. At another level, Aquinas could use the philosophical language of Aristotle to speak of marriage as an arrangement of mutual comfort and friendship between equals. At a lower level still, he could use the naturalistic biological observations of Aristotle and later commentators to explain marriage formation among humans as a natural process. It came about, he claimed, because of the long period of human infant dependency that required the labors and investments of both the biological mother *and* the biological father.

This double language was, to a certain extent, lost in the Protestant Reformation. Or, to be more accurate, law, philosophy, and theology became more differentiated during that period. Theology centered itself more completely on the language of the Bible. Law assumed and depended on visions of faith but more and more developed its specialized legal and philosophical language. But the double language was never completely lost. Luther and Calvin retained aspects of Aristotelian naturalism. For instance, Luther in his famous *The Estate of Marriage* (1522) could, on the one hand, say that marriage was an ordinance of God commanded at creation and, on the other, sound like a modern utilitarian and say that if a woman has a baby out of wedlock, "she will become poor."

Public policy about marriage and family in a pluralistic society proceeds primarily at the level of naturalistic and philosophical argument. There is little doubt that the language of health and the language of economics—how marriage and family policies will affect the health and economic well-being of both individuals and society—are now the central language for public policy. It is also clear that those who come to these debates out of explicitly religiocultural heritages must also learn to understand and to some extent use this language. But the analysis of even our most stripped down and apparently neutral languages of health and economic well-being demonstrates that wider background assumptions inevitably undergird the actual use of these naturalistic and philosophical languages—assumptions that resemble the logics of religious visions and faiths. These background assumptions often project visions of the trustworthiness of life, its regularities, its larger purposes, or perhaps even the fundamental ways life is aggressive and egoistic or warm and empathic. The evidence supporting the validity of these broader assumptions, even within so-called secular thought, is weak when measured by narrow scientific canons, rendering the casual affirmation of these assumptions similar to the explicit faiths of historic religious communities. Insofar as this is true, faith and unfaith, the secular disciplines and religious traditions, are closer bedfellows than is generally assumed.[50] For these reasons, people of faith and people who consider themselves secular must have more charitable attitudes toward one another in public debate; they are more alike than they often realize.

These wider visions and background assumptions surround, contextualize, and give meaning to narrower debates over the facts, even in human sciences. The field of psychology alone offers plenty of examples. Organic and harmonistic views of the ultimate context of reality run throughout the humanistic psychologies of Maslow, Rogers, Jung, and even the more recent work of the psychoanalyst Heinz Kohut. This is why in these psychologies we can trust our self-actualizing tendencies; in the end these psychologists hold that all true self-actualizations are compatible and in harmony—quite an assumption (or should we call it a faith?), but hardly a matter of strict science as such. Freud saw human experience as the scene of a huge struggle between the cosmological forces of life and death. The behaviorist B.F. Skinner had a mechanistic view of reality and so do the so-called selfish gene theories of much of sociobiology.[51] But these larger images of the ultimate context of experience have more the character of faith-like hunches than tested empirical truth. Yet they color interpretations of the empirical facts. On this score, secular disciplines such as these and religious traditions are on even ground; the explicit arguments in public debate advanced by both are surrounded by broader background assumptions for which neither side can give accounts on narrowly rational grounds. The background beliefs—the faiths, so to speak—of the ostensibly secular arguments are often more difficult to discern, but they are there and functioning nonetheless.

In light of this, diverse religious and secular perspectives can often strike agreements by finding analogies between their respective traditions at more practical levels of debate. Almost all of the so-called axial religions have within them a more differentiated language that permits them to enter into complex conversations with other perspectives. Both Islam and Judaism, as did Christianity, had its own romance with Aristotelian philosophy, helping all three to develop this differentiated language. Furthermore, the exegetical and interpretive endeavors of all traditions with literary heritages help produce the kind of differentiated language that facilitates participation in public debate. For those traditions that were primarily oral such as some Native American traditions, we must encourage a new generation of competent scholars and interpreters to represent their insights for public dialogues as they tend to proceed in a primarily literary society. There is now evidence that such a new generation of interpreters of Native American traditions is emerging, and it is now time for society to learn to listen to their voices.

An example of how a tradition can become more differentiated and, therefore, more able to take part in the complex debates of modern societies can be seen in how Islam, at least in many countries, has given up its earlier practice of polygyny. Geoffrey Parrinder (1996) points out that much of the justification for plural marriages in the Qur'an is associated with the need to preserve the property of orphans whose fathers had been killed in battle. One way to do this was for a Muslim man to marry the orphan's mother and provide her with a dowry that would endow her and her offspring. But it was also necessary, according to the Qur'an, to treat all wives fairly. In view of this requirement, the practice of polygyny has been renounced by many leading Islamic scholars.

Parrinder writes:

> In modern times some Muslim apologists have claimed that, while polygamy was permitted in olden days, and under special circumstances, yet it is impossible to act fairly or "with equity" towards several women, and men should therefore marry one only. Thus the Qur'an is quoted in favour of monogamy.

Some scholars recently have demonstrated that all of the world's great religions have ways of asserting and defending basic human rights for both men and women.[52] But they do this in different ways and have effectively implemented these rights only to varying degrees.

For the most part, the classic religions introduce what we have called "intrinsic moments" into thinking on marriage and family. By intrinsic moments we mean ways to interrupt and limit the chain of instrumental justifications for the goods of life, including those of marriage and family, whether they be primarily based on health or economics. In the West, these intrinsic moments have had to do with the good of children (their intrinsic value in contrast to their usefulness); the sacred worth, dignity, and autonomy of both husband and wife as contracting agents; and the sanctity of the marital commitment (the vows, covenant, or sacrament). These intrinsic moments were variously seen as based on commands of God, analogies to the action of God or the gods, or as part of larger teleological aspirations toward the good and the true. Religion is not the only way to ground and justify these intrinsic moments; Kantians have anchored them on an understanding of the rationality of persons and what this requires for treating them as ends and never as means only. Nonetheless, religious traditions have been one of the most profound and durable ways of securing them.

These intrinsic moments should in principle be recognized in a public philosophy and public policy. Utilitarian logics of health and wealth are informative, but they *must* have their limits. Within the context of more encompassing intrinsic values about the status of persons, children, and covenants, the logics of health and economics have their rightful but subordinate place in analyzing and justifying the goods of marriage and family. Just how this double language will work itself out on specific issues will vary. Our argument has been that both public policy pertaining to the state and public philosophy pertaining to the wider society need an understanding of both languages. This is true even though, to some extent, public policy in its marriage and family talk will specialize in the language and logics of health and economics. But those languages and logics, while they have their place, must also have their limits.

6

Directions: Culture and Civil Society

We now turn to more specific directions and solutions. In so doing, we will move from culture to systems to personality. This chapter will continue the cultural explorations of the last chapter. In chapter seven, we will examine the massive systems of government and market. In chapter eight, we will return to persons—mothers, fathers, children and ways to address their family needs. Of course, although these three foci can be distinguished, they should never be separated in actual social practice, even though for the sake of clarity that will appear to be what we are doing. Remember: it gets to the heart of our thesis that these three spheres should and can cooperate to address marriage and family adequately in our day. This affirmation gets to the core of our public philosophy for families.

We no longer live in sixteenth century Germany. Although this is where church and state found some degree of differentiation and where the state's interest in families was most decisively established, the Reformation never viewed the state as a strictly secular sphere as we do today. The church still had pervasive influence on the state in ways that it does not, cannot, and should not today. The Declaration of Independence and the First Amendment lay down the rules governing the relation of religion and the state for the U.S. These rules have implications for the development of a public philosophy for family and marriage.

We agree with those scholars who like to interpret the meaning of the First Amendment against the background of the Declaration of Independence. There is some validity in understanding the First Amendment words "Congress shall make no law respecting an establishment of religion, or prohibiting the free exercise thereof" in light of the Declaration. The Declaration of Independence tells us that "We hold these truths to be self-evident, that all men are created equal, that they are endowed by their Creator with certain inalienable rights, among them are Life, Liberty and the pursuit of Happiness." Reading the First Amendment from the view of the Declaration suggests that although the state should neither establish nor prohibit the expression of religion, it should have a generous and enabling attitude toward religion. Why is this so? Because assumptions of a religious kind established in the Declaration the ground of human equality and rights. This is the meaning of the words "endowed by their Creator." This is why many experts believe that the Constitution is not completely neutral about religion, even though it establishes no particular religious faith. The two of us agree with those who hold that the First Amendment permits a positive relation between government and religious institutions as long as the state does not establish a specific religion nor prohibit the free exercise of any one religion.

This position is important for our argument. In order to accomplish our vision of renewal for the American family, there must be a cooperative relation between religion and state, between the various institutions of civil society, and between market, state, and civil society.

Intermediate Principles

In chapter 2, we listed some common affirmations that emerge from taking seriously the classic traditions that have shaped American life and the newer ones that are beginning to express themselves today. We now want to organize them more clearly around the diagnostic categories set forth in chapter 5, i.e., the cultural, social systemic, and psychological causes of family disruption. First, in response to the cultural forces of individualism and their interaction with technical rationality, we recommend the reassertion of a variety of intrinsic values often best carried by our religiocultural traditions—the intrinsic dignity and worth of both husband and wife, the intrinsic worth of children, the importance of marriage for family formation and childbearing, the sanctity of the marital contract or covenant, the importance of both fathers and mothers for children, and a cultural appreciation for the transcendental claims that traditions have used to buttress and support these intrinsic values. To counter individualism and technical rationality (and the cultures of divorce and nonmarriage that they have produced) requires, we believe, a grand cultural work—one involving multiple strategies by different spheres of society. But crucial to this cultural work will be the reclamation and reformulation of our classic marriage and family traditions—both the old ones that have principally shaped Western culture and the newer ones with which we must now enter into dialogue.

Second, at the social systemic level, we must address the pockets of debilitating poverty that still destroy many families. Governments often try to eliminate poverty by showing its economic costs to the entire society. Functional and utilitarian justifications are increasingly advanced as reasons for helping poor families. But, once again, such pretexts for helping poor families are never enough and must never stand alone. We also must support and enable poor families for more intrinsic reasons—because of their status as humans, however particular traditions may justify this status. Furthermore, work and family issues must be addressed at this social systemic level. This initiative is often justified as a matter of market self-interest—the needs of business for happy, healthy, and relaxed workers. But society should also solve work and family tensions on grounds of the intrinsic

worth of both husbands and wives and the implications of
the ethic of equal regard for a just distribution of their respective rights, responsibilities, and privileges.

Then there must be solutions at the psychological level—
at the level of the human person in relation to others. This
is where we will emphasize the emerging new programs in
marital education and communication. Once again, these
programs are important not only because they lower the
blood pressure or improve the sex life of couples, but because marriage education may be a method for implementing intersubjectively the classic principle of love as equal
regard, i.e., for implementing *concretely* love as mutual respect and active helpfulness.

The Role of Religion

It is dangerous to start with the role of religion. It risks
communicating that marriage and family issues are mainly,
perhaps only, the responsibility of church, synagogue,
mosque, and temple. We are not saying this. But we do believe that religious institutions, as they did in the past, have
much to do with providing the *commitment* language for marriage and family—a language that can, we hope, include but
also enrich the functionalism that dominates public policy
debates about marriage and family. Even before the language of commitment seeps into the nooks and crannies of
public policy discussions—and it inevitably does and
should—it shapes the more diffuse spheres of civil society.

So, here is our first piece of advice to religious institutions—*learn your heritage on marriage and family.* For many
parts of modern religion, this heritage has been forgotten.
We believe that this is a shame. Since one of us has recently
led a large scholarly investigation of the religious contributions of Western family and marriage theory, we can assure
you that the effort to reeducate ourselves and our religious
institutions is well worthwhile. But even then, learning these
traditions does not mean avoiding the task of critiquing
them.

A new culture of marriage and parenting must first arise from the voluntary institutions of civil society. Religious institutions are the dominant expressions of civil society. But they are not the only institutions; civil society takes many forms. The field of marriage and family exhibits a huge assortment of voluntary organizations; some of these are community based organizations (CBOs) that work primarily at the local level. We will describe many of these organizations below. But civil society and the voluntary sector is a massive field of human action. We can make our points only by giving illustrations of a few important programs that exemplify our general principles.

We will speak first about the emerging religion based Community Marriage Policy and its extension to include secular institutions and government. We already have learned something about Judge James Sheridan's Community Marriage Policy that has developed common standards for both religious leaders and secular professionals dealing with marriage. It is actually, however, an extension of journalist Michael McManus's Community Marriage Policy.[53] Over a decade ago, McManus became troubled by the mounting evidence of marital and family disruption in our society. He also was convinced that the churches he knew—mainly Protestant churches—were not doing enough to address the problem. In searching for solutions, he discovered the Common Marriage Policy of the Roman Catholic Church, a program followed by nearly all dioceses throughout the country. This common policy has several components: a six-month preparation period, the administration of a premarital questionnaire (PREPARE or FOCCUS), the use of mentoring couples with the engaged and newly married, the use of marriage preparation classes (Pre-Cana workshops, Engaged Encounter, Marriage Encounter), and engagement ceremonies before the entire congregation. McManus has adapted this model and tailored it for ecumenical use as a Community Marriage Policy for religious institutions throughout the country. Churches in over 100 communities have adapted some form of the policy as have several communities in England. Although no controlled studies have been done on their effectiveness, many communities have experienced declines in divorce rates, although a strict causal relation between community marriage policies and fewer divorces has not been established. Such studies have yet to be done.

What interests us most, however, is the extension by Judge Sheridan of this concept to include the marriage and family professionals, both religious and secular, of an entire community. This is a genuine effort to create a common marriage culture. This idea has been adapted by an even more ambitious program called The Greater Grand Rapids Community Marriage Policy. The program, begun in 1997, has the following objectives: to reduce by 25 percent the number of failed marriages, to reduce by 25 percent the number of children growing up without the benefit of a mother and father living together, and to make thorough premarital preparation a community norm. Doctors, ministers, teachers, therapists, professors, and university presidents helped establish the policy and are working together to implement it. It has many of the same features of McManus's program but now held and implemented by a much wider representation of the community. Changing the culture of the community on marriage and family is the central goal—hence, the use of conferences, seminars, lectures, workshops, and even announcements pasted on billboards with such words as "Strengthening Marriage . . . Supporting Children." Multiple justifications for this program have been advanced by its leaders. These include appeals to the health values of marriage (Professor Waite has lectured there) as well as to traditional religious sanctions of marriage based on the ideas of covenant and sacrament. Different parts of the community have different reasons for supporting the policy, but, as we have suggested, they find *analogies between their different languages, and this is enough for the purposes of a rough communal consensus.* Research on the project by the Couples and Marriage Policy Resource Center, Calvin College, and the Annie E. Casey Foundation is now underway, but final reports have not been completed. The Grand Rapids experiment, however, strikes us as bold and creative. It is primarily aimed at changing the culture of marriage in the Grand Rapids area, but it is doing this partially by changing the relation between the various professions and the way they deliver their services.

There is room in the Grand Rapids experiment for the double language that we have been urging—the language of health and economics *and* the language of commitment based on the intrinsic values, symbols, and narratives of the faith traditions. The leaders and workers in these programs use both languages. From our standpoint, this double language—this bilinguality—may be the most important part of this program and mark it more as a "cultural work" than simply a technical exercise in better marriage education and communication. We think the existence of both languages in justifying and guiding these programs is creative as long as one of them does not drive out the other. There is evidence, in fact, that in Grand Rapids, with its strong Dutch Reformed population, the language of commitment provides an important encompassing context for psychological and educational languages often used for communicating with professionals who have been socialized to these languages in their training. On the basis of our interviews and firsthand knowledge, we notice that leaders in Adrian and Grand Rapids have detectable religious commitments on marriage and family even though they speak to the public primarily in terms of the functional values of these institutions. These leaders have difficulties using in public the language that captures their deeper religious commitments. In our day, the language of commitment is elusive.

Another program illustrates, with some scientific rigor, the advantages of using the tools of marriage and communication education within religious institutions that have more intrinsic understandings of the importance of marriage and family. We have in mind the research done by Howard Markman and Scott Stanley at the University of Denver around their communication education program called PREP (Prevention and Relationship Enhancement Program).[54] Markman and Stanley have evidence that the context within which PREP is administered makes a difference to its effectiveness. Their simple but well-researched Speaker-Listener technique has more lasting effects when administered within faith based institutions than it does when presented in a secular clinic. This technique—which trains couples to allow the partner to speak without interruption, to listen, to paraphrase, and to speak for oneself—sinks in more deeply when learned within a supportive religious community that has a deep history of symbolism about and commitment to marriage and family. This is a marvelous example of one of the meanings of our view of biculturality—the use of insights from modern psychology within a larger context of history and tradition.

Some readers with empirical tastes may be asking for specific data. What evidence is there that cohesive religious traditions make a measurable difference in marriage and family life? Before giving a sampling of the data, we ask the reader to remember this: our argument primarily has been philosophical. We are not advancing a theological or confessional argument. We are not advocating a particular religion so much as examining how its language of commitment based on intrinsic values may help resist, or at least balance, the prudential justifications of marriage based on health and economic well-being. If many religions use a language of commitment that gives expression to intrinsic moments, what evidence is there that this makes a difference?

Here is a sample of some of the empirical evidence. For instance, according to data assembled by Call and Heaton, the rate of divorce is 2.4 times higher in marriages where neither spouse attends religious services regularly than for those marriages where both wife and husband attend every week. Attendance is also associated with higher marital satisfaction and skeptical attitudes toward extramarital sex.[55] In their massive study of American sexual behavior titled *The Social Organization of Sexuality* (1994), Laumann, Gagnon, Michael, and Michaels reported that those couples who frequently attend religious services are only one half as likely to divorce as those who do not attend. From another angle of vision, Bumpass and Sweet have data showing that single women under age thirty-five who never attend religious services are nearly twice as likely to cohabit as those who attend on a weekly basis.[56] And finally, another recent study shows that men who attend services regularly are half as likely to commit partner violence than those who attend once a year or less.[57] These correlations are suggestive. Might they be associated with the languages and symbolisms of commitment and self-control found in many religious bodies? And if so, doesn't this warrant the new move to bring marriage education and religious institutions into more fruitful collaboration?

The Role of Civil Society

But religious institutions are not the only players in civil society. There are many other organizations with explicit interests in family and marriage—all the way from the National Council for Family Relations, the Family Resource Coalition of America, the Children's Defense Fund, the newly formed Coalition for Marriage, Family, and Couples Education, and the well-known conservative Family Research Council and Focus on the Family. Although we do not always agree with the positions of any of these organizations, in the grand scheme of things, each has a role to play. There are, in fact, dozens of generally secular voluntary or nongovernmental organizations addressing family issues. They exhibit the insight held in Western societies since the Reformation, i.e., that marriage and families are valid concerns for the common good and can be seen to be so both from a religious and a secular point of view.

All of these organizations face the fundamental cultural dilemma of how to balance strengthening intact marriages with the genuine needs of single-parent families and step families. *Our view is that cultural energy should first be put into creating more intact marriages and families. This, however, should be done without neglecting the needs of disrupted families.* Cultural work should first of all be spent on increasing the number of stable marriages and the families that they establish. These initiatives should come first from the spheres of civil society. Although government and market can join in this reconstructive process, leadership must come from the voluntary sector. It is in recognition of this belief that we have spoken more about a public philosophy for families than merely of a governmentally based public policy.

We want to illustrate our points by discussing a special part of civil society—the grass roots community based organizations that are mindful of the unique culture of the people they serve. We want to describe Avance, the organization that one of the authors, Gloria Rodriguez, founded. Both of us think it exemplifies much of what we are saying at the more abstract level about the role of civil society. Avance is a family support, parent education, and early childhood agency that functions throughout the southern regions of the U.S. It delivers its supports within a context of explicit cultural assumptions; it affirms the strengths of traditional Latino culture and helps its clients to both reaffirm and reformulate that cultural tradition. It is also dedicated to bilinguality and biculturality. It believes that young Hispanic and Latino children should learn both Spanish and English. They should learn the former in order to stay in contact with their extended families, culture, and history. They should learn the latter to negotiate the modernization process. This leads us to the meaning of biculturality; Avance believes that successful work with Latino families involves helping them to live in two cultures. This means being well enculturated into the traditional culture that extends back into history for generations as well as socialized to the emerging culture fueled by science, technology, and market rationality. There are tensions between these two cultures, but this is good. Out of this tension may come mutual critique and correction.

Both cultures have their strengths, but they need each other. Both cultures carry different kinds of "social capital," to use a well-known phrase coined by the eminent social scientist James Coleman. Traditional culture carries with it a string of intrinsic values that resist commodification and the nearly unbroken chain of means-end utilitarian values that dominate so much of contemporary public life and discourse. These values, in the Hispanic context, include strong marriages, two-parent families, the sacred worth of children, the importance of honest work, and the importance of community. These values and virtues have not customarily been taught because they "pay off." They are generally presented as enduring virtues and values that are worth internalizing and living by even when *they do not appear to be maximizing our immediate interests.* These more tradition based values, from the standpoint of Avance, are both guides to coping with modernity and checks on its excesses. Yet, as Coleman pointed out, such values function as social capital anyway; they are not justified and learned for their functional value, but they nonetheless help societies increase their utilitarian satisfactions. To put it bluntly, Avance is a value-laden, not a value-neutral, social service agency, and it is this without apology.

Avance, however, is not a church. True, Roman Catholic values permeate much of Hispanic culture, but it is these values as culture rather than as doctrine, confessional dogma, or tests of fellowship that inform Avance's work. And there are more distinctively Hispanic values that it celebrates as well. In many ways, Roman Catholic moral values function as "classics" (in the sense that we earlier defined the word) that have proved trustworthy over the centuries. Furthermore, Rodriguez believes that some of the classic or central values, i.e., the importance of the equal-regard marriage and the value of children, have been informed as well by the early Aztec civilization that also runs through some expressions of Hispanic culture; hence, they have enjoyed multiple sources. Not only has historical experience demonstrated them to be classic, in the sense of being durable and reliable sources of insight, but also modern scientific research of the kind reviewed in chapter 3 is giving them new plausibility.

Avance is fully informed by the social science research we summarized above—research that shows the overall negative consequences of divorce and nonmarital births and the goods of intact marriages for health and economic well-being.

But, once again, Avance is bicultural. It does not allow the functional language of the social sciences to dominate its culture and the culture of its clients. Through cultural celebrations, observances of special holidays, the use and honoring of the Spanish language, and a general attitude that respects the symbols and traditions of Hispanic culture, it helps its people live in two worlds, with the stronger emphasis on the importance of received traditions.

In many ways, Avance fully illustrates the theoretical point we made in the opening chapter. The social sciences cannot alone give us the foundations for family life, childbearing, or marriage. These must come out of traditions—albeit traditions that are continuously refined. But they can clarify certain ambiguities within our traditions, provide limited critiques, and help their adherents gain flashes of insight that aid in their reconstruction. We realize that it is a long way from the practical, everyday activity of Avance and the theoretical resources of Wittgenstein, Gadamer, and Ricoeur that we used to make this point in the early chapters. Good theory leading to good practice can be found in many places, not necessarily only within the pages of the formal books of philosophy.

Avance helps marriages mainly by improving parenting and family communication and providing embattled families with community supports. The pressures of the fast-paced, digitally driven U.S. society on poor Latino families are enormous; they function to undercut many of the latent strengths of this historically cohesive culture. Avance concentrates on helping parents. It does this by going in two directions at once. In its nine-month parenting courses, Avance gives young mothers and fathers insights into the importance of early stimulation for proper brain development and insights into the developmental regularities of childhood learned from Erikson, Piaget, Kohlberg, and others. But it also reminds these parents of their traditional strengths and helps them learn and appreciate them even more deeply. Improved parenting helps improve marriages, and stronger marriages make for better parenting. Avance also strengthens marriages by creating better supports from the community as a whole. Parents and families who belong to an Avance chapter learn to organize as communities to provide mutual support and solve problems—especially threats to their children from gangs, guns, and drugs. They build parks, organize play for children, develop crime-watch programs, organize couples support groups, and support schools. In fact, in some communities, Avance serves as a bridge or link between schools and families. This doubtless is a sign of the future. Either community based organizations will help close the distance between schools and parents, or schools themselves will expand to perform a variety of family support functions. Our society must learn to bridge the gap between home and school; one or the other of these models—and in some places both—must be pursued.

Avance is up-front about valuing marriage, but it also relates to and helps all families—single parents by divorce or nonmarital birth and step families. It cautions couples about the hasty use of divorce to solve marital problems, but it acknowledges that divorce is sometimes necessary. Single parents need parenting education even more than two-parent families. And single-parent families and step families need to relate to the resources of tradition and the wider community even more than intact families. Social isolation, according to McLanahan and Sandefur, is a major threat to the well-being of disrupted families. Churches, synagogues, and mosques can bring great resources to overcoming the possible social isolation of single-parent families and step families. But culturally sensitive and community oriented social service organizations can often provide similar services and sometimes in more focused ways.

Avance is fortunate to have earned a high profile. It gets financial support from government, local organizations, businesses, churches, and foundations. It exhibits one of our major points—the importance of interlocking cooperative efforts between civil society, the state, schools, and the market. But the very fact that it illustrates this kind of cooperation between the various spheres of society makes it a good example of the problems that such cooperation also quite often brings with it. These problems and challenges will be discussed in later sections of the book.

We have chosen to illustrate several of our more theoretical points by a rather extensive analysis of Avance. We know that there are many such nongovernmental or voluntary organizations serving a variety of groups—African American, Asian, Islamic, and, indeed, mixed groups from a variety of backgrounds. Our points about Avance apply to many other similar initiatives. We could have described the important multisector cooperative work on marriage and family developing in the state of Oklahoma under the leadership of Jerry Regier and Governor Frank Keating. We could have referred also to the complex cooperative project of First Things First—a community based organization serving Chattanooga, Tennessee. These efforts illustrate a new trend toward helping fragile families go two directions at once—toward deeper roots in some cultural tradition and toward greater skills to deal with modernity.

The Professions

But there are other manifestations of civil society—other than religious institutions and nongovernmental social service agencies—that greatly affect marriage and family. Take, for instance, the professions.

Our commentary on the professions, marriage, and the family will be limited in scope. We will pursue only one question, although many are worthy of our attention. What should the professions do with the new knowledge, summarized in chapter 3, about the on average negative consequences of marriage and family disruption and the positive consequences of marital and family stability? More specifi-

cally, how should the professions handle the new information, as qualified as it is, put forth by the Amatos, Booths,
Popenoes, and Waites of this world? Should this information
inform their practices and, if so, how? The ethics of professional practice—whether the profession be law, medicine,
education, therapy, or ministry—are always formed in part
by the moral values of the communities they serve. This is
right and good. But it is generally believed that the professions also should serve the interests of the persons who seek
their services. Sometimes, however, individuals and families
who seek professional help do not always have access to the
full knowledge that might inform their choices.

This brings up the question: do the various professions
have the obligation of giving this information to those they
assist? Even more than that, do they have the obligation to
help their clients, patients, or congregants work through
this information in light of the full dynamics of their deci-
sion-making processes? To put it more pointedly, do the professions need to be pro-marriage and pro-family, or at least
mildly or gently so, within certain constraints? We think that
the answer is "yes, they do," but with qualifications.

This is an enormous topic. At best, we can only illustrate
points that might be relevant for a wider range of profes-
sional-ethical concerns than we can tackle here. We will confine ourselves primarily to the psychotherapeutic or
counseling professions that address issues in family life and
marriage. For decades, there has been a fiction within the
psychotherapeutic disciplines. This fiction propagated the
belief that psychotherapy was strictly a science and therefore
neutral about values. Hence, on issues pertaining to marriage and family, counselors and therapists should be value
free and nonjudgmental, i.e., follow the lead of clients and
help them realize goals within their own values, whatever
they might be.

Although there are many good discussions of this issue,
the recent writings of marriage and family scientist William
Doherty are among the best. In his articles and 1995 book titled *Soul Searching: Why Psychotherapy Must Promote Moral Re-*

sponsibility, Doherty shows how much of marriage and family therapy became captured by an ethic of individual fulfillment. He writes, "Claiming neutrality on commitment and other moral issues in American society meant that the therapist likely embraces the reigning ethic of individualism."[58] This ethic of individualism often leads therapists to disrespect marital commitment on the part of clients and indirectly induce pro-divorce behavior on the part of clients. Doherty tells the example of a therapist who once told his client to "trust" her feelings and to admit that "you are not happy in your marriage." When the client protested that she loved her husband and was "committed to him," the therapist responded, "The choice is yours, but I doubt that you will begin to feel better until you start to trust your feelings and pay attention to your unhappiness." Doherty believes such words indicate that the therapist was not just neutral but subtly nudging his client toward separation. Furthermore, when this woman fired her therapist and turned to her priest, his advice was mixed. On the one hand, he cautioned her to make certain it was not her depression that was causing the marital problems rather than the other way around. That was good advice. But then he added that there was the possibility of an annulment "if the marriage was causing the depression." Doherty reports that the woman was "even more stunned than she had been by the therapist." Here we have two professionals, therapist and minister, who may be tilting their advice toward individualistic values, and in the process avoiding or short-circuiting the underlying psychodynamic issues. The fact that one of these professionals was a minister should not surprise us. One national survey revealed that pastoral counselors were the least cautious of any of the sub-professions of marriage counselors when it came to the advisability of divorce for couples, even when children were involved.[59]

There is some evidence, however, that marriage and family therapists may be somewhat less individualistic than Doherty thinks. This same national survey of the ethics of professional marriage and family therapists indicates that there is a thin yet important ethic of relationality—an ethic governing the rules of intersubjective communication—that many marriage and family therapists and counselors are trying to promote.[60] This is not a complete marriage and family ethic, but an important one, especially for couples and families who may be having major communicative difficulties in the first place. Nonetheless, Doherty's major concern is well-taken. Do therapists have a moral responsibility to help clients think through the meaning of their commitments and the consequences of their actions to others as well as to themselves? And does part of that responsibility entail informing clients of the probable, even though not certain, consequences to others and self of marital dissolution? Doherty thinks there is such responsibility, and we do too.

We have illustrated the question of the ethics of the professions in dealing with marriage and family issues by turning to marriage and family therapy and counseling. We also could show similar issues facing the professions of law, medicine, education, and even business as a profession. These professions stand as powerful forces in civil society that not only affect our lives directly but exert strong influence on cultural values in general. The professions help us define our ideals of family life and marriage. This part of their work may be even more important than what they actually do within the confines of the consultation room and the counseling hour.

Our request is not that the professions override good judgment about the welfare of their clients. But we do urge that they embark on the cultural work we have called for—a critical conversation designed to determine just what their moral responsibilities are to marriage and family as both private relations and institutions of momentous public importance.

7

Directions:
Government and Market

Cultural renewal proceeds first from the creativity of civil society. Grass roots movements such as Mothers Against Drunk Driving (MADD), the Sierra Club, or Common Cause gain transformative power because they build on the imagination and energy of average people with passionate commitments to vital causes. We must start here to build a new culture that encourages and supports marriage and families. Recognizing these truths should be part of a public philosophy for families.

But cultural traditions and cultural creativity also interact with the great systems that shape our lives, e.g., government and market. Indeed, there are many ways in which these systems both reflect culture and themselves generate culture. To speak of government and market as systems is simply to point to the various ways in which institutional patterns themselves organize life in ways that are at least quasi-independent of the cultural values they also embody.

Even though cultural transformation comes primarily from the institutions of civil society, there is much governments can do to encourage and support both marriage and family—but never without mandates and help from the tradition-preserving and reformulating powers of civil society. Furthermore, there is much the state can do to cooperate with civil society, regardless of which takes the lead. And finally, there is a great deal that governments can do to both regulate and cooperate with the market for the good of families, and possibly even the goods of marriage.

In what follows, we will investigate a few of the myriad of possibilities open to government.

Government and Culture

First, government—its administrative, legislative, and legal bodies—must be sensitive to the diverse cultures that make up the publics it serves. This means that governmental family policies should evolve mainly from the legislative wings of government—not primarily from the courts nor the back rooms of government agencies, administrators, and staffs. Legislatures are that part of the state most in tune with average citizens and the traditions that have formed them. Many of the lasting conflicts in American life over family issues have arisen because the legislative process has been by-passed. As frustrating as it often proves to be, it is more trustworthy in the long run. Governmental family policy cannot simply be left to academic, legal, and bureaucratic specialists. We say this without throwing aspersions on experts of any kind, be they legal, economic, sociological, or psychological.

Our point is more philosophical, one that we have made from the beginning of the book. The analytic and explanatory contributions of experts help clarify and sharpen the wisdom of deeper cultural traditions, even though these traditions themselves must undergo continuous revision. We agree with sociologist Alan Wolfe: governmental policies should grow out of and reflect the free and open discourse of civil society. We fully realize that civil discourse and the legislative process must function within constitutional constraints, but for the most part these are the places where public policies on family and marriage should be established.

This observation leads us to our first general principle pertaining to government: *the state should do nothing to impede or short-circuit free deliberation and free expression of opinions on matters pertaining to marriage and family by people in their daily lives in civil society.* This is the basic level at which a public philosophy for marriage and family must develop. Public policy should reflect the evolving public philosophy of the voluntary institutions of civil society.

This leads us to our second general principle. Government should do nothing to obstruct the free *critical retrieval of our marriage and family traditions. For example, it should not, in searching for a language of individual rights or one about the health consequences of various family arrangements, inadvertently develop an alternative official language that replaces the languages of commitment carried by our religiocultural traditions.* For instance, government should be reluctant to enshrine the jargon of "costs and benefits" in talking about marital relations, "investment" in speaking of parental love, "trade-offs" in speaking of the tensions of family life, "negotiations" when referring to marital contracts and covenants, and "satisfactions" when speaking of the goods of marriage and family. Government and the laws it makes should be equally cautious about the excessive use of the language of rights, another popular and useful language but one that can displace more traditional languages of commitment. Although primarily addressing the sphere of government expressed in family law, legal scholar Carl Schneider makes a point applicable to the entire range of the state's influence. Both state and family law should "move away from the atomizing language of rights to a more encompassing language of relationships, responsibilities, and contexts." They also should be more willing to use the "language of morals and less anxious to substitute for it alternatives like the language of medicine, psychiatry, and economics. Family relations are, among other things, ultimately moral." Unless the moral aspects of those relations are taken into account in the language they use, government and law "will be poorly equipped to understand what people are doing in family relations. And the strength of the family as a social institution lies in central part in the moral obligations family members assume toward each other. For the law to ignore those obligations is for it to weaken that institution."[61] Or to say it differently, if narrow social science languages or narrow philosophies of rights provide the only languages of government and law, then these sectors of society may function unwittingly to undercut the public use and plausibility of traditional languages of commitment.

As legal scholar John Witte (1997) has argued, the development of Western marriage and family law has been a complex interweaving of at least four different languages. There has been a *naturalistic* language that conceptualizes the various impulses and needs that marriage and family organize. There has been a *contractual* language that has been the special province of law and government. There has been a *religious* language that, in the West at least, generally used the language of covenant and sacrament. And there has been a *social* language that conveyed the value of marriage and family for the whole of society. In recent years government language increasingly has narrowed to the contractual language of rights or the naturalistic language of health and economics. But government and law should do its best to keep alive a fuller language. It will even be better and more accurate in its use of the languages of contract, health, and economics if it is hospitable to the reinforcements of social and religious languages, i.e., the languages of commitment.

Welfare and Workfare

The Work Opportunity and Reconciliation Act of 1996 ended Aid to Families with Dependent Children, a program that guaranteed federal cash assistance for poor families. This new legislation was designed in large part both to strengthen poor families and reinforce the institution of marriage. Welfare to families is now administered under a program called TANF (Temporary Assistance to Needy Families) and principally gives assistance to poor families as they make the transition into work. Block grants have been given to the fifty states to devise programs as they see fit, under certain federal guidelines. In place of a uniform national program, we now have a patchwork quilt of different state programs.

Within two years after the reforms were implemented, welfare rolls had declined; just under 8 million people remained on the rolls, down 44 percent from 14.3 million in 1994. Many observers believe that this has been an accomplishment. In the case of the two of us, Browning agreed with Senator Daniel Moynihan: the old system was broken and needed fixing, but a new national welfare system was required, not fifty programs going in many different directions. Rodriguez was in 1996 more open to the move toward federally funded state programs if they, in turn, truly supported the work of CBOs. Anchoring welfare with CBOs was her main concern, not moving welfare to the states as such. It fit her belief that welfare needs to be administered by those close to the people served; if state governments support CBOs, fine, but this might also be done by the federal government. But she also holds that whether it is the fifty states or the federal government that administers the money, programs need to provide entitlements for the desperately needy and develop dependable and predictable funding patterns for the CBOs used to accomplish much of the actual work—something that happens all too seldom.

We both now agree that welfare reform has had some significant strengths. But we also believe there are problems and that significant improvements are required before welfare reforms can be called a success. First, requiring welfare parents—generally mothers—to find employment only works if child care is available, affordable medical insurance is provided, the mother can afford transportation to work, job training is given when needed, and actual jobs are available. The new welfare is working best in those states—Wisconsin, Indiana, Michigan, and Minnesota—where these kinds of supports are in place. In fact, recent studies done on the TANF program in Minnesota by the Manpower Demonstrating Research Corporation reveal surprisingly promising results when these and other supports are in place. In that state, parents can obtain paying jobs, continue food stamps, and keep 38 percent of cash welfare money for every dollar earned by the outside job. The proportion of welfare recipients with jobs has risen by 35 percent and earnings have increased by 23 percent for each person working. Most notable was the increase in marital stability, with domestic abuse declining by 18 percent and marriage rates increasing by 50 percent compared to persons on traditional welfare. Child well-being increased as well. Whether we have a national welfare system or a variety of state programs, if such statistics hold, it is very likely that other states will imitate aspects of the Minnesota program.

We applaud President Clinton's proposals in his year 2000 State of the Union address to meet these needs with additional federal dollars—$150 million for job training for fathers, $430 million for housing vouchers, $150 million for transportation to work, $18 billion over five years for child-care tax credits, and $1.3 billion over five years to restore health care and food stamps for immigrant families. These funds should help provide some of the additional supports that workfare requires.

But there is a second concern. Independent of the need for care for younger children, the emphasis on work does not provide for the supervision of the older children of poor families, especially the children of single parents. Researchers are presently attempting to determine if there is an increase in the number of children in foster care because some welfare parents can no longer cope with the demands of both full-time employment and the supervision of their children. Furthermore, unsupervised children are more likely to join gangs or get into trouble in other ways.

Third, there is the issue of jobs, both their availability and their stability. Even in the good times since 1996, employment for untrained welfare parents is difficult to find. The "digital divide" that we mentioned above is a huge obstacle and can only be solved by education and job training, if even that will address the problem. The instability of much low-paid work means that even for those who do find a job, it often does not last for very long. A truly serious attempt to address the needs of poor families cannot neglect this fundamental issue.

Lastly, there is the issue of marriage itself. Welfare reform was created to encourage marriage, or at least not to discourage it as the older AFDC was thought to do. But few steps actually have been taken to accomplish this goal. Only recently have some states discovered that TANF funds can be used for programs that encourage marriage among welfare recipients. For instance, early in the year 2000, Governor Frank Keating of Oklahoma designated $10 million dollars of TANF money to be used for marriage education. Supporters of marriage education were elated; marriage was finally being officially acknowledged as an antidote to the poverty of single mothers and encouraged with programs funded by federal dollars. But the question soon arose: how can marriage education be targeted and made effective with the truly poor and disadvantaged? Would this money be soaked up by the middle classes—not entirely a waste, perhaps, but at the expense of other important TANF programs aimed principally at the poor?

This concern raised an issue first brought forth by Theodora Ooms of The Resource Center for Couples and Marriage Policy. Can the tools of the new marriage education movement be adapted for use with the poor and with minority groups where the need is highest? Can minority churches and religious institutions be vehicles for early and effective education for marriage, communicative competence, and conflict resolution? We would add, can religious institutions be effective sources for the poor of both marriage education *and* powerful symbols of commitment? It is our conviction that they can be; in some churches located in low-income communities, this is already happening. In fact, research by Browning on Chicago inner-city black churches shows that some of them make marriage education with both engaged and married couples central to their overall ministries.[62] There is little doubt, however, that the goals of the 1996 welfare reform act to encourage marriage cannot be accomplished through welfare-to-work programs alone; more intentional strategies must also be used.

Families and Taxes

We applaud the new public interest in how taxes affect marriage, family formation, and family well-being. As we write these pages, a healthy new bipartisan debate is occurring on how to make national tax policies more family friendly. All parties to the discussion—both conservative and liberal—seem to agree; it is now time to reform tax programs that discourage marriage, and it actually may be appropriate to actively use taxes to encourage marriage. But the principles and values guiding this discussion are far from settled.

It is widely agreed that there are various tax measures that directly or indirectly damage marriage. These are of two kinds: 1) penalties resulting from the progressive tax system that bring couples with combined incomes into higher tax brackets, and 2) penalties, mainly affecting the poor, resulting from supports such as earned income tax credits, food stamps, or housing supplements that may be phased out when two modest salaries are combined at the time of marriage. This latter kind of penalty is extensive and affects many people (including the widows of servicemen) during the transition to marriage. These two sets of difficulties are pervasive. They are excellent examples of how technical reason in the form of bureaucratic rationality can, as Jürgen Habermas would say, invade "the life world" and dislocate its customary patterns.[63] Such interruptions have led tax expert Eugene Steuerle to write:

To remove most marriage penalties . . . requires reconsideration of practically the entire shape of our transfer and tax systems. This tail literally would wag the dog, or perhaps more precisely, one can't take the tail somewhere without bringing along the whole dog.[64]

In fact, this is the main point that we want to make on this topic: it is time for a systematic review of the effects of tax policies on families and marriage. Tinkering here and there will not do. Although it may be time to take a small step such as addressing the marriage penalty because it seems politically possible at this moment in history, more sweeping action sooner or later will be necessary. We must soon examine the "whole dog," as shaggy and unkempt as it may be.

Here are the principles that should guide this new grooming and manicuring. *First, we should no longer apologize for using tax measures to support both family and marriage.* To support these institutions through taxation is no different in principle than using tax codes to support economic development, home buying, retirement savings, and the purchase of medical insurance. It has been well established that tax policies rightfully can be used to support families with children. Both tradition and recent social science research testify loudly that marriage, on the whole, is good for children— but also for adults. Why not use tax programs to support the institution of marriage itself? Furthermore, marriage and family have been ravaged by the other form of technical reason we wrote about in chapter 4—the whiplash of market forces. Can't tax programs be used to tilt the balance in the other direction by supporting marriage? In short, we are arguing for a humane reformulation of bureaucratic rationality expressed in misguided tax policies to help correct a misguided market rationality in the form of bad work and family relations.

Such reforms, however, will not unfairly privilege marriage. As Steuerle points out, the economies of scale enjoyed by marriage (thought to be the main reason married couples are often taxed at higher rates) are also enjoyed by other shared living arrangements such as "dormitories, old age homes, movie houses, and cohabitation." He goes on to say:

Yet, in practice today, marital vows of allegiance are the only type of arrangement that is taxed. In those communities where marriage is no longer the norm—and these communities are growing—this natural social incentive to achieve economies of scale in living arrangements does not disappear, but merely is converted in forms that void the marriage contract.

Second, beware of flat and unimaginative applications of justice. It sounds good to say that singles and married couples should be taxed equally. But this can overlook many concrete realities that real justice must keep in mind, e.g., the financial vulnerabilities of moving from singleness to married life, the expense and demands of child rearing, the importance of children to the common good, and the cost of raising children to parents' employment and long-term career development. Real justice must keep these special factors in mind.

Third, some tax benefits for marriage should be aimed at the institution itself; others should be directed primarily toward its child-rearing aspects. We protect and support marriage partially because it is an important and vulnerable institution. But it is an institution with many functions, a principal one being the conception, support, and socialization of children. Yet, as is the case with all institutions, people use marriage for a variety of purposes, and many use it who cannot or will not have children. Therefore, some types of tax support for marriage as an institution must apply without regard to how specific couples use it. Other supports, however, should be targeted more specifically to its child-rearing tasks as such.

Fourth, with regard to supports that are specifically targeted at the child-rearing functions of marriage and families, we should not discriminate against any one group of parents. We should help families where both parents work outside the home and families where one or the other remains home to care for the children. We should support needy single parents with children at home, no matter how they became single parents—whether through divorce, nonmarital births, or other kinds of hardship.

These general principles lead us to make the following suggestions. Since history is in the making on some of these proposals even as we write, we offer them more to illustrate their general relevance than to influence immediate debate. Marriage penalties due to the progressive tax system should be softened. We think that income splitting is the best method to accomplish this goal. Rather than taxing couples on their combined income, the total amount earned between them should be split into two equal parts and each taxed on one half of their total income. A couple where one makes $15,000 and the other $35,000 should not be taxed on $50,000 but on $25,000 each. Furthermore, we recommend adjusting phase-out penalties so that poor people moving into marriage do not simultaneously suffer the losses of such supports as food stamps, income tax credits, and Medicaid while also getting taxed at higher rates. Such measures will, we believe, help support marriage as an institution among the poor.

But even more specific steps should be taken to support married couples raising children. These steps would be universal and apply to all adults with legal responsibility for raising children—single parents, step parents, grandparents, and gays and lesbians raising children. The recently passed $500 a child tax credit was a major step forward and we commend it. But even then, it fell short of the recommendation by the National Commission on Children (1991) chaired by John D. Rockefeller IV. It recommended "the creation of a $1,000 refundable child tax credit for all children through age 18." This is not simply a progressive proposal from liberal political voices. Bill Mattox, formerly of the more conservative Family Research Council, has publicly recommended increasing the child tax credit to $1,500. Furthermore, in another report, the Family Research Council has argued that the tax exemption for children, now at $2,750, should be raised to $8,200, where it would be today had it kept pace with the rate of inflation. It is shocking to think that this is what the child exemption would be if it had the same value that it did when first created roughly a half century ago. We authors do not push these numbers as experts who have done all the advanced arithmetic; we have not. We place them before the reader to point out that interesting and provocative proposals do exist from a variety of knowledgeable persons and groups—proposals that need to be part of the American debate over the family.

Finally, we are sympathetic with those who claim that the present Dependent Care Tax Credit is unfair. This provides up to $1,440 to parents in the wage economy who use commercially based child care. As it stands, this can be used only by employed parents and not by families where one or the other parent provides the care. Many people believe this provision, obviously needed by some families, is also discriminatory toward couples who decide to sacrifice a second income and handle child care themselves. We agree with those proposals arguing that the Dependent Care Tax Credit should be made fixed, universal, and evenly applied to all parents—perhaps $700 or $800 per child, regardless of whether the child receives commercially based care.

Government and Health

It would be pretentious for us to offer solutions for one of the major issues facing American life today—the cost of medical insurance and the absence of affordable insurance for literally millions of American families. But it must be kept alive as an issue to be solved. Not only is good health fundamental for families and affordable access to good health care a basic human right, they are also crucial for the solution of another major problem that confronts American families—the growing tensions between work and family life. This is an issue we will discuss at length later in this book. If, as we will argue, our society must have more flexibility in the workplace so that employed parents can have time at home with children and each other, we need more part-time positions that also receive the supports of adequate health insurance. Some very basic system of universal health care would seem to be the answer—a system to which supplemental private insurance plans could be added. But such plans have been much discussed and generally rejected by those with political power in our society. This leaves us with a major problem that this book can only highlight but not solve, i.e., the need to continue to make progress with this profound problem, either by piecemeal additions to existing programs (as seems to have been the recent strategy) or by some more comprehensive and universal plan (which seems out of favor at the moment).

Law, Marriage, and Family

We will conclude our discussion of the role of government with a few words about family law. All modern societies have laws regulating aspects of marriage and family; many ancient societies did as well. Even as cohabitation and the deinstitutionalization of the family progress, family law adapts and in many ways has continued to spread its influence. How many young men are stunned to learn that when their girlfriend becomes pregnant, they may be forced *by law* to make child payments for years whether married or not and whether they did or did not have a role in deciding whether to have and keep the infant? How many couples fully understand that child payments made by the nonresidential and never-married parent are *by law* equal in many states to those required by a divorced parent? The law can spread into our lives even as we think we are making decisions to stay clear of legal entanglements. The present paradox of cohabitation and the deinstitutionalization of family is this: *at the same time that people believe that they are avoiding the law, they are against their will actually becoming more embedded in it. It escapes many people that the uncoerced decision to marry is also the decision to elect the protections of the law, and to do so freely.*

The many pressures moving our society toward the deinstitutionalization of family cannot be effectively countered by the legal mechanism of family law. As Carl Schneider says, law is a "blunt instrument" for the task of reinstitutionalizing the family. In recent decades, the law may, in fact, have been

better at contributing to its deinstitutionalization than its re-
institutionalization. According to Schneider, one of the most
telling ways that law has contributed to family deinstitutionalization is through creating a variety of "functional equivalents" to marriage, such as legal procedures for settling
disputes between cohabitors (Marvin vs. Marvin) or the creation of legal domestic partnerships.[65] The problem with
these functional equivalents is that they undercut the dis-
tinctiveness of marriage. The strength of marriage as an institution is partially found in its uniqueness in relation to
other institutions. Its special character has been found in its
intentionality, the commitment brought to it, its presumed
permanence, and its status as a freely chosen institution. To
quote Schneider again, "The functional-equivalence approach seems to equate relationships which will often lack
these special qualities (indeed, which will sometimes have
been chosen exactly to avoid them) with relationships which
do have them." We believe that the legitimate problems that
domestic partnership laws are designed to address—insurance needs, visitation rights, rights of inheritance—should
be solved through other methods. We take this stand not to
deny these privileges to gays and lesbians as such; we will address issues related to them in the last chapter of the book.
Rather, we do it to help halt the increasingly blurred distinction between marriage and nonmarriage among the great
mass of heterosexual couples. It is, we believe, one small way
in which family law can contribute to the reinstitutionaliza-
tion of family and marriage.

   Although law is limited in what it can do to reinstitutionalize marriage and family, it does have the power to formu-
late models that guide our image of marriage and family as
institutions. These institutional models, as Steven Nock argues, help people know what they are aiming toward when
they get married and form families.[66] They free us from the
perplexing burden of creating anew our own self-crafted institutions—institutions that invariably lack wider community
support because they are not recognized and understood. It
is better to learn the competencies required to enact a rea-

sonably successful and well-known marital pattern than to create *de novo* something that has never been seen or tried. Legal definitions of marriage and family provide templates that can be learned, but they do not in themselves create the motivations, values, or commitments that lead people to pursue them. It is our conviction that legal models of family and marriage should have a considerable degree of consistency with the cultural and religious models that have led people in the past, and often still do today, to want, value, and be committed to the institutions of marriage and family—even if these models need reformulation.

Nonetheless, family law has additional basic contributions to make to rebuilding families. Many of these pertain to the requirements for entrance into and exit from marriage. We believe that some new options pertaining to entrance to marriage are very promising. There are several ideas afloat. Some experts would lengthen the time between applying for a license and the marriage itself; they believe that the longer a couple knows each other the more likely it is that the marriage will survive. Some states, such as Florida, are inducing, not forcing, couples to take marriage education courses by lowering the license fee and shortening the waiting period for those who do. Arkansas is considering giving a tax break to couples who take such courses. Minnesota passed a law to cut the license fee by $50 if a couple takes a twelve-hour premarital class, but Governor Jesse Ventura vetoed the bill. At last report, it may be overridden.

Covenant marriage laws covering both entrance into and exit from marriage are even more ambitious. Both Louisiana and Arizona have passed such laws; other states have tried but so far failed. In Louisiana, two types of marriage now exist—one covered by regular no-fault divorce and another called covenant marriage that requires higher standards for both getting married and getting divorced. Couples *elect* a covenant marriage; it is not forced upon them. They agree to undergo premarital counseling, seek marital counseling if problems develop in the marriage, and can only seek divorce for adultery, commission of a felony, abandonment by the other spouse, addiction, separation for two years, or cruel treatment by the other. We believe this innovative experiment has several positive features and is worth being adopted, and perhaps refined, by other states. It is not coercive. It emphasizes the seriousness of marriage and promotes marriage preparation. It encourages counseling when couples are in trouble, yet it does permit divorce even though the requirements for it are more stringent. Although only 3 percent of Louisiana couples have chosen covenant marriages, consciousness about marriage has risen in the state, religious institutions are taking their role in preparation more seriously, and some impulsive marriages have been discouraged.

Covenant marriage can be viewed as a variation of the idea of "super vow" marriages—an idea developed by legal scholar Elizabeth Scott and promoted by communitarian Amitai Etzioni. Marriages with super vows permit couples to draw up their own individual contracts that heighten the standards for divorce. Both ideas, but especially the covenant marriage concept, take steps to tilt the modeling power of the law in a new direction and open possibilities for reconnecting marriage law with classic traditions of marital commitment. But since covenant marriages are chosen, not required, it accomplishes these values without forcing traditions of commitment on those who do not understand or want them.

This brings us to the specific topic of no-fault divorce. There is now evidence that the move from fault to no-fault divorce in the 1970s actually contributed to the increase of divorce, although this evidence is not undisputed.[67] In contrast to some theories that said no-fault laws only permitted many bad marriages to finally end, some argue that these laws had a "demonstration effect" (were suggestive and showed the way to divorce) and lowered "investment" in marriage ("since marriage is so unstable and easily dissolved, why expend the energy to make it last?"). Furthermore, as we have seen, there are negative consequences for both children and women due to divorce. This is especially true—as we saw above—for the majority of divorces that seem to involve relatively low levels of conflict. No-fault laws permitted more or less unilateral divorce and made marriage contracts among the most easily broken contracts in our society, often to the great disadvantage of both mother and children.[68] As one state governor has said, possibly with some exaggeration, it is "easier to get out of a marriage with children than it is to get out of a Tupperware contract." *Although both authors of this book fully acknowledge that there is a place for divorce within our society's marriage system when cruelty, addictions, and irreconcilable differences exist, there is also good reason to believe that we have often too readily used it as a method for solving marital conflicts.*

In view of this situation, there are many serious proposals to reform the present system of no-fault divorce. We believe some of these are worth considering. They constitute one more small step in the complex task of replacing the culture of divorce and nonmarriage with a thoughtful and reconstructed culture of marriage. One of the first and most elegant voices promoting a children-first policy was that of legal scholar Mary Ann Glendon of Harvard University. William Galston of the University of Maryland and Katherine Spaht of Louisiana State have carried her suggestions forward by proposing the replacement of the no-fault system with a legal system that slows divorce, protects women, and puts children first. Galston's plan goes like this. No-fault laws would continue to apply to those couples without children who divorce by mutual consent. But for those with children, it would no longer be used. Couples with children divorcing by mutual consent would be required to observe a waiting period and undergo some counseling. But more important, they would be required to file long-term financial plans covering the needs of their children until eighteen or possibly even twenty-one, if college was likely. The details of these long-term plans would have to be settled before other divisions of property between the adults could be settled.

Legal scholar Katherine Spaht, one of the authors of the covenant marriage legislation in Louisiana, would go even further with the children-first principle. She proposes extending the legal concept of community property, in which both husband and wife have equal rights to existing wealth, to the idea of family property. The latter concept would mean that, in principle, the value of the total family wealth would belong equally to all family members, including the children. At the time of death or divorce of parents, the current value of all wealth would be divided equally. For children, trust funds would be established until they become adults. This is a radical yet creative extension of the children-first principle. It sends a strong message about the nature of marriage and family as the creation of a covenant community. It is a recent proposal that has not been thoroughly evaluated. But it illustrates the possibilities of a new way of thinking about divorce law that puts the welfare of children much more centrally into the picture. It is, in principle, the kind of creative thinking that needs encouragement.

In conclusion, government takes many forms and all are limited in what they can do to support marriage and families. Nonetheless, when orchestrated in relation to initiatives and resources that come from civil society and the market, government can be one important factor in the total cultural work needed to reinstitutionalize marriage and families. We now turn, however, to the market.

Market, Marriage, and Families

It is proper to treat government and market in the same chapter: they both represent powerful expressions of what Habermas calls "the systems world." Both impinge upon everyday life and civil society, often for the good and often in disruptive ways. Government can render us passive and, through its various services, turn us into clients with little control over our lives. Markets can pull us into their competitive and efficiency driven logics, pull us away from our homes, and infect us with ways of thinking that, when taken back to our families, tempt us to think of spouses and children in analogy to balance sheets, where only the rules of costs and benefits apply.

Nonetheless, none of this is inevitable. Governments can do much to humanize market and protect families. Government can protect families by establishing minimum wages, minimum ages at which young people can be employed by certain industries, and standards for basic insurance packages so necessary for family health. The state protects the rights of employees to be represented by labor unions. Some of these unions have been interested in family wages and decent working conditions for fathers and mothers. During the last decade, we have seen the passage of the Family and Medical Leave Act (1993), which guarantees parents time off from work, without pay, to care for newborn children. We have seen its extension to provide time for parents to visit their children's schools. And some people would like to extend parental leaves for childbirth to include pay—an idea very much worth further research. All of these steps are examples of government as a system protecting family and parents from the overbearing power of another system—the market. All of this is for the good. How far government should go in protecting families is a matter for careful judgment. But it is self-evident and essential, in our view, that the state has an obligation, through duly elected representatives of the people, to play such a role.

There are limits to what government can do to regulate the market's relation to families. Just as government is limited in what it directly can do to revitalize families, it is also limited in what it can do indirectly through the regulation of the market. Because we believe this is true, we consistently have placed the central initiatives for family renewal within the institutions of civil society.

There is one very big step that the market must take to help families and remove the pressures it places on marriage. This involves finding ways to reduce the amount of time that parents work outside the home in the wage economy. Business should take this step primarily on its own with little nudging from the state. It is entitled to take this step out of self-interest. We agree with Amitai Etzioni, however, in believing that even the marketplace has more than one motivation. As he argues in *The Moral Dimension* (1988), even the business community can make, when clearly confronted by powerful public discussion, judgments about intrinsic goods and basic rights of individuals and families that transcend mere cost-benefit calculations.

So, what should businesses do, regardless of the motives that make them do it? They must create more flexible work hours so that couples with children will not deprive their offspring of needed parental care and presence during the crucial years of their development.

We have heard of the many small steps that industry is taking in this direction—more flex time, more shared jobs, more work that can be done at home, more child care at work, more time for sick days that can be used for children, more time for school visits and teacher conferences, and longer vacations. This is all well and good. And it is encouraging to notice that in the present competitive environment for competent employees, industry is virtually showering such perks on workers. *But the big idea is this: American society needs to develop the social system and the supporting culture that make it possible for a husband and wife with children to put no more than a total of sixty hours a week in the wage economy.* This time could be split between husband and wife as they see fit, although this idea should not be interpreted to sanction one partner working the full sixty hours while the other remains home with child care and domestic duties. Whether the sixty hours are divided forty-twenty, forty-five–fifteen, or thirty-thirty would be a judgment made by the couple in light of their respective skills, inclinations, and the possibilities available in their specific circumstances. But American society should make a concerted effort to create the values that would support this idea and the social conditions that would make it possible. More flex time, part-time jobs, and shared jobs would be needed. To move in this direction, we also will need, as we mentioned above, more and better medical insurance covering all the new fifteen-, twenty-, and thirty-hour jobs created to make the sixty-hour work week possible. Furthermore, *the sixty-hour work week is, we think, a concrete implementation of the love ethic of equal regard.*

There is a small but meaningful amount of research that indicates that the sixty-hour work week for a couple with children brings with it a wide range of additional satisfactions. A pilot research project that came from the Harvard University hospitals found that couples who had some kind of sixty-hour-a-week arrangement enjoyed a wider range of satisfactions than those who either worked a total of eighty hours or those where one partner worked full time and the other stayed home. The single-career households had more time, but the one partner who remained home missed the stimulation of a job and ended up doing a disproportionate amount of child care and housekeeping. On the other hand, when both husband and wife worked full time, they had little time for each other or for the children. But in the sixty-hour homes, couples had more time for each other and the children than the eighty-hour arrangements and shared housekeeping and child care more equally than those couples where only one partner worked full time.

We think this study is suggestive, but it is not large enough to be definitive. It gives us further reasons, however, to inquire into the idea of the sixty-hour work week for couples with children. The same principles have implications for single parents who are either well employed or on welfare. There need to be more well-paid and well-insured thirty-hour jobs for single parents. And workfare also should be tied to the idea that single parents should not work outside of the home for more than thirty hours.

We are not recommending that our entire society move to the sixty-hour week. This is not our point. But it does seem possible, especially in this computer age, to develop the employment flexibility needed to provide many more fifteen-, twenty-, and thirty-hour positions so that the sixty-hour week becomes a genuine possibility for couples with children. We remind the reader that, although we are not recommending a universal thirty-hour work week, one major company—the

Kellogg industries—did in fact institute a successful thirty-hour work week during the 1930s, 1940s, and 1950s. It both functioned well for the company and was appreciated by employees. It was finally terminated, not because it was not successful but because the expanding economy of the 1950s tempted breadwinners to earn more.

To create the sixty-hour week will require a work of culture as well as the reorganization of our market systems. The energies bringing about this work of culture must spring from the families, neighborhoods, organizations, and churches that make up civil society. These are the places where the time deficit is most acutely felt. Nonetheless, the market, sometimes with the nudging of government, must find a way to provide for this new pattern of work in the wage economy. Such a move will create a stimulus for mothers, fathers, and children to redefine the meaning of marriage and family.

It is to these individual persons that we turn in the next chapter.

8

Directions: Persons

Marriage and family are about many things and can be viewed from multiple perspectives. But, in the end, they are about persons—mothers, fathers, children, grandparents, uncles, aunts, and cousins. Families are both carriers of culture and formed by the culture that surrounds them. The institutions of civil society—churches, synagogues, clubs, neighborhood organizations, schools, and families themselves—are the major carriers of this culture. And there is frequently a religious dimension to much of this culture. Families are also parts of other social systems—government and market being two of the more powerful. So far, we have restricted our analysis and recommendations to culture and social systems.

Now we must turn to the persons themselves who make up families. No matter how powerful the culture or how influential the systems that pattern our lives, persons are active centers of agency and communication. Persons are constantly synthesizing their experience and responding with initiatives that are much more than the sum of all the discrete influences that play upon them. If persons are not themselves learning to be active centers of synthesis, agency, and communication, even the most benign cultural and social environments may produce people unable to handle the challenges of marriage and family. This explains why people who have been socialized within extremely pro-marriage and pro-family environments sometimes get divorced just like those who grew up in less supportive contexts. They received good messages, good symbols, good traditions, and even good local supports but did not learn to take active and communicative command of what they were given. The reverse is also possible. A few rare individuals with poor cultural supports and who seek marriage and family on individualistic grounds may do well in these institutions because they also have the communicative and synthesizing skills needed to handle their tensions.

Of course, the best of all worlds is to have all three—strong cultural traditions, supportive social environments, and good processing and communicative skills to handle the conflicts of close relationships. The first two without the third may often fail, especially within the context of rapidly modernizing and globalizing societies such as our own. But the third (communicative skills) without the first two (culture and supportive social environment) will be equally destined for frequent disappointment. The task of a public philosophy and policy for families, and the cultural work that it entails, is to hold all three together.

Marriage Education

In our analysis in chapter 4 of the causes of family disruption, we showed how the interaction of cultural individualism and market forces undercut traditional supports undergirding marriage and family life. We argued that because of these trends, marriages today thrive when the couple itself has the requisite commitment and skills. Let us now address the second factor—the matter of skills. More and more, these skills are being seen as *communicative skills*, i.e., the skills needed to communicate love and equal regard, to communicate one's wants and intentions, and the skills required to handle interpersonal conflict. There is the growing belief that these skills *can be* taught, and there is increasing confidence that they *should be* taught. With regard to this last point, one frequently hears these experts say that marriages do not endure because of an absence of conflict; they stay together because the couple learns to manage conflict through their communicative competence.[69]

Intentional marriage education addressing communicative issues has been in existence for several decades. The Roman Catholic Church has been a leader in marriage education. Its Marriage Encounter weekend that the Spanish priest Father Calvo designed in the 1960s has now become ecumenical and is called Worldwide Marriage Encounter. It was influenced by a prior marriage education model called Cana and pre-Cana, marriage education programs that were principally focused on teaching the specifics of the Catholic view of marriage as a sacrament. But from its inception in the 1960s, Marriage Encounter aimed more at facilitating communication and sharing between couples. It was built around weekend retreats for married couples during which spiritual lectures were alternated with couples writing letters to one another in the privacy of their rooms and dialoguing about the meaning of their communications to one another. In its early days, as many as 100,000 couples a year in the U.S. alone experienced Marriage Encounter weekends. Surveys of couples taking these weekends show that they are highly valued and widely thought to have helped their marriages.

But Marriage Encounter is generally thought not to emphasize training in communicative skills in the way typical of the newer research based marriage education programs. Evidence showing that the newer programs are superior is recent but beginning to mount. Over the last two decades there have been several impressive investigations, of an explicitly scientific kind, into what makes for satisfying and enduring marriages. Some of these research programs have been located in major universities and received large grants from the U.S. Institute of Health and other sources. For

years, the results of these investigations have been buried in
social science journals. Recently their findings have been
published in more accessible books and promoted by professional organizations and other bodies.

Most notable are those studies by Professor John Gottman
of the University of Washington, Professors Howard Markman and Scott Stanley of the University of Denver, and Professor David Olson of the University of Minnesota. For
instance, Markman, a former student of Gottman's, has
joined with Scott Stanley and worked on the details of communication in a premarital and marital program called
PREP (Prevention and Relationship Enhancement Program). Olson is known for the development of an inventory
and education program called PREPARE/ENRICH, the first
a premarital assessment and the second a marriage enrichment inventory. Olson's premarital inventory is based on national norms developed from giving the instrument to
350,000 couples. The inventory claims to be able to predict
with 85 percent accuracy those couples who will stay together and those who will divorce.

It is on the basis of these new resources, and the aura of
science that surrounds them, that the state of Florida has
passed a law mandating marriage education courses for high
school students. It also encourages engaged couples to take
a four-hour premarital course by lowering the marriage license fee for those who do. The covenant marriage states actually require such courses for those electing a covenant
marriage. It is also on the basis of the claims of the marriage
education movement that Australia is extending its state supported premarital education programs. A similar move toward state supported marriage education and counseling is
occurring in the Blair Labor government in England. Other
countries have their own adaptations of these programs, for
example Australian PREPARE/ENRICH and FOCCUS Australia, the latter being a Roman Catholic inventory first de-
vised in the U.S.

These programs are promising; they constitute one dimension of the complex cultural work that will be required

to restore marriages and families to vitality and health. However, we expect it to be someday clear that, as important as are the skills they teach and the predictive power of their questionnaires, these programs help marriages and families because they convey a high valuation of these institutions. They help create a "culture of marriage"—a sensibility among people that marriage is important and that good marriages are possible. In short, they take marriage seriously, communicate this to the public, and convey hope. For decades it has been shown that new therapies are more effective when they are first invented, partially because their creators have such faith in them and convey it to their clients. Something similar may be true with the new marriage education. There is a high degree of belief abroad that they are effective, even though evidence for long-term effects is still tentative. Nonetheless, it is our conviction that when used within communities where high levels of commitment to marriage already exist, they can make a significant additional contribution.

Although the different marriage education programs vary from one another in small details, they are more alike than different. In what follows, we set forth our own synthesis of common themes that run through the literature of marriage education. Their major point, as indicated above, is this: marriages stay together because couples learn how to handle conflict. Marriage education is about learning how to do this. This does not mean that successful couples necessarily solve the problems producing their conflict. The couple establishes, however, a mode of communication that does not damage the self-cohesion or self-esteem of the other partner, and the two of them develop a pattern that integrates them as they work on issues in an ongoing way. Second, marriage education helps couples to communicate in such a way as to produce more positive over negative messages. In fact, according to John Gottman's electronic surveillance of the physiological patterns of communicating couples, good marriage communication has five times more positive than negative responses.[70] The third common feature is ownership of one's messages; in good marriage communication, couples express their own individual thoughts rather than mindreading the other or ascribing negative motives to the other while defending oneself. Holding and validation are the fourth themes; one need not always agree with one's partner, but one must validate the other's feelings and words and support or "hold" together one's partner's sense of self-cohesion, even in the midst of serious disagreement.

There are additional features that deserve discussion. The first has to do with a major conflict in the field of marriage education. Some marriage communication experts—such as Markman and Stanley (1994), and Harville Hendrix (1988)—believe that active listening conveyed through empathic rephrasing of the partner's communications is central to good marital communication. Gottman and his associates, who themselves once subscribed to the importance of active listening, now discount it as the crucial glue that holds marriages together. They arrive at this conclusion because their laboratory observations have taught them that couples do not often use active listening and paraphrasing and that, when partners do use them, they do not correlate with long-term positive results. Gottman believes that rather than active listening making the difference, it is two other factors—the percentage of positive over negative responses that couples have achieved in their communication and the skills that they have acquired in negotiating conflict.[71] Gottman, Markman, and Stanley *do* agree in believing that men become more physically aroused by negative communications than women and for that reason more readily withdraw or become aggressive in face of conflict. In view of this asymmetry between men and women, a good marriage is one in which the wife learns to state her negative responses gently and the husband learns to be influenced by his wife's point of view. But Markman and Stanley decidedly disagree with Gottman over the importance of active listening; they continue to hold to the importance of active listening and have had energetic and useful public exchanges with Gottman defending their point of view.[72]

We do not need to follow this debate to its conclusion. Indeed, it does not as yet have a conclusion. And that itself is significant. *If the alleged scientific claims of marriage education are part of the grounds for governments supporting it, and if, in turn, these claims are unclear, is public policy getting ahead of itself in encouraging, and sometimes requiring, marriage and relationship education?*

To answer this question, we must return to the beginning of this book. There we argued, with the help of several schools of contemporary philosophy (ordinary language analysis, hermeneutic philosophy, and certain forms of American pragmatism) that neither public philosophy nor public policy can ever be grounded on strictly scientific grounds. Furthermore, the social sciences probably will never achieve the kind of exactitude characteristic of the physical and biological sciences. Hence, in the realm of human affairs, we must justify action on wider grounds, using the social sciences as consultative rather than exclusive and determinative resources. *If we expand the public support of marriage education, this decision will be based on reasonably plausible scientific evidence for its usefulness, not settled scientific judgments. We will need the confidence that our various traditions also tell us something about marriage, something about good preparation for it, and something about effective communication. In short, we must believe that we have the collective good sense to put such initiatives together.*

The marriage education movement should be seen as analogous to the discussion within political philosophy of what Jürgen Habermas (1990) calls "discourse ethics," the rules and skills governing communication for solving problems and facilitating joint action. As societies become more differentiated and pluralistic, we must all learn more fair and effective ways of communicating—in business, in government, in everyday practical relations, but first of all in marriage and family. In fact, in order to have communicative competence in business and government, we need to first learn what good communication means in the home. This is an insight taught by philosophers from Aristotle to Aquinas to the contemporary liberal feminist Susan Moller Okin; all of them believe ethical and effective communication radiates outward from the home to the wider society. We believe that marriage education is, when rightly understood, an effort to bring discourse ethics—the ethics of fair and open communication—into the sphere of intimate relations. We believe it is a way to improve our intersubjective skills in understanding the other from his or her own point of view as we also help the other come to know and hear our own thoughts and feelings. Developing "communicative competence"—another term from Habermas (1976)—in a variety of fields will be a prominent agenda in our society for the future. We see no reason why marriage and family should be excluded from this more general educational trend, and we can imagine many reasons why it should gain the approval of a public philosophy undergirding public policy.

Marriage education, as important as it is, cannot stand alone in its effort to restore good marriages and healthy families. It will work best when used within a context of strong and clear justifications for marriage already present within the surrounding culture. Since our society appears to have difficulties appropriating our historically classic justifications for marriage, many people today are tempted to turn to newer ones coming from the social sciences. For instance, marriage educators often justify their commitment to marriage on a variety of grounds. Some take a market approach: since 95 percent of Americans want a happy marriage, marriage educators try to give people the skills for, as the title of Harville Hendrix's popular book says, *Getting the Love You Want.* Others advance justifications that are, in the terms of moral philosophy, more broadly teleological in logic. In short, they argue, as we already have seen, that marriage is a means to other ends, i.e., that marriage on average is good for the persons involved (their health, their sex life, their wealth), that it is good for society, or that it is good for both the individual and society.

These narrowly social-utilitarian or ethical-egoist appeals are enormously attractive to people in a secular age. They are also attractive to the professions of law, medicine, and psychotherapy that feel uncomfortable with their classic religious, moral, and philosophical groundings. Justifications for addressing marriage and family issues built on "what people want" or what contributes to their well-being enable these professions to publicly justify their work in ways that the older rationales seem unable to achieve in the current social atmosphere. We should be reminded, however, that these prudential and social-utility justifications always have had some place in the Western religious tradition, although generally a subordinate one.

A generous public philosophy for marriage and family will find ways to orchestrate the two languages—the languages of health and the languages of commitment. Roman Catholic marriage theory always has spoken of the health and comfort goods of marriage and family; but it anchored these goods in the notion of God's will for creation and saw individual and social health as dimensions of the higher quest to enjoy the good of God. Even Luther and Calvin saw marriage and family as social goods, but ones that first of all reflected the ordinances of God. Judaism and Islam took much the same approach building, however, the grounds of these institutions on the idea of covenant. Warrants for marriage and family as positive contributions to community health can be absorbed into and recontextualized within the traditions of the Western religions and probably also within the classic Eastern religions as well. This needs to happen if marriage and family, viewed as community health measures, are to resist being reduced to mere cost-benefit calculations—on the same level as the purchase of automobiles, insurance, footwear, and public utilities.

Marriage and Family Education in Schools

The marriage education movement will not by itself save marriage, nor will it alone revitalize families. It will make its contribution most effectively when seen as one part of a larger, multifaceted work of culture. Some marriage educa-

tion programs take this turn. In a recent review by Dana
Mack (2000) of marriage education programs for high
school students, she is most impressed with those that ac-
quaint students with the classic religious, philosophical, and
imaginative literature on marriage and family. This is the nature of the curriculum called *The Art of Loving Well* developed at Boston University. This successful and
well-researched program is presently used by schools
throughout the country. It combines both readings and
some exercises in communication. A new anthology on
courtship titled *Wing to Wing* (2000) brings together many
of the great philosophical, religious, and social science writings on the evolution of marriage and family institutions.
The latter book does not employ the tools of relationship
and marriage communication. The two of us believe that the
best programs will combine the two approaches, i.e., the retrieval and reformulation of our classic marriage traditions
and growth in communication skills. This hope follows from
our view that reflective reimmersion into our classic marriage and family traditions can go hand-in-hand with insights from the social sciences, even research based
perspectives on marriage communication. Bringing these
two resources together is central to the cultural work we en-
vision.[73]

Another program that begins to approach the balance between communication education and attention to classic
marriage and family traditions is *Connections* (1996), written
by Charlene Kamper and distributed by the Dibble Fund.
This fifteen-week course is used in high schools throughout
the country and will soon be available in a version suitable
for use in religious institutions. It combines exercises in relationship communication and practical problem solving in finances, child care, and family decision making with
introductions to basic concepts about the meaning of marriage, parenting, and family.

There are other more traditional approaches to marriage
and family education in high schools and colleges that must
not be overlooked. There are textbooks written on these

subjects for both high school and young college-age students. These texts, often used in introductory social sciences courses, not only convey social science facts about marriage and family but also paint general images and ideals about the meaning and purpose of these institutions. There is now active controversy, however, about their scientific adequacy and the viability of the cultural images that they project. The distinguished University of Texas family sociologist Norval Glenn released a report in the autumn of 1997 assessing the current college-level textbooks. The report was titled "Closed Hearts, Closed Minds: The Textbook Story of Marriage," and it attracted so much interest that it was republished in a variety of contexts. In this report, Glenn severely criticized almost all of the texts then in use in nearly 8,000 courses and read by thousands of students who probably viewed them as authoritative. According to Glenn's analysis, these texts tend to ignore the known benefits of marriage, generally depict marriage as oppressive, downplay marriage as an institution, overemphasize the amount of child and spousal abuse associated with marriage in contrast to informal relationships, and hide or de-emphasize the known individual and social costs of divorce and out-of-wedlock births.

An assessment of high school texts by New York University psychologist Paul Vitz tells a somewhat more optimistic story. His report, titled "The Course of True Love" (1998), shows that texts at this level depict marriage more positively and are more balanced in the range of topics that they address. Nonetheless, they justify marriage and family primarily in terms of what they contribute to individual self-actualization. They fail to review the deeper cultural, religious, and legal traditions shaping the formation of these institutions in our society. Is there a problem with the moral tone of these texts? There may be. Most moral philosophers argue that self-actualization, all by itself, is an inadequate justification for either moral action or social institutions; social conflict, especially in intimate relations, can seldom be solved if the partners involved believe that the actions of both self and other are always and only motivated by what he or she believes is personally fulfilling. Self-actualization as a moral principle and motivation cannot alone solve conflict; it can only hope that through some lucky eventuality, the self-actualizations of two different people will be congruent or that one of the individuals will capitulate to the fulfilment of the other. It cannot be the moral and cultural grounds for marriage and family.

To sum up, we believe that good materials, courses, and texts for high school and college-level teaching are an important part of the cultural work needed to rebuild families and marriage. These courses will be most powerful when they combine attention to classic traditions with communication education and the social scientific analysis of these institutions.

Fathers

In chapter 4 we summarized evidence for the growing disconnection, through divorce and nonmarital births, of fathers from their children and their children's mothers. There has been some resistance to recognizing the individual and social costs associated with fatherlessness. For instance, in 1992, the legal scholar Richard Posner in *Sex and Reason* declared that there was no evidence that fathers were essential to children and families if their income could otherwise be replaced. As recently as the summer of 1999, *The American Psychologist*, the official journal of the American Psychological Association, carried an article advancing a constructivist philosophy of the social sciences and criticizing all attempts to assert that family form, including the presence of fathers, was important for the welfare of children. According to the article, it was the quality of the relation, not its form, that made the positive difference for children.

As we argued in chapter 3, thanks to the research of Amato, Blankenhorn, McLanahan and Sandefur, Popenoe, Snarey, and many others, we now have evidence that family form, the two-parent family, and the presence of fathers do contribute to the well-being of children. This is true partially because the quality of relationship is also likely, on average, to be better in two-parent families where fathers are present, and also partially because investments of energy and time are more enduring in such families.

Practical social movements also have contributed to this new concern about father absence. Ken Canfield's National Center for Fathering was one of the first training and education programs designed to increase the skills and commitment of men to the task of fatherhood. As early as 1988, Avance recognized that it needed marriage and parent education for fathers as well as mothers; if mothers advanced and left fathers behind, this was destructive to the marriage. In the autumn of 1994, Don Eberly and Wade Horn—with the blessings of bipartisan national leaders such as William Bennett, Al Gore, and William Galston—started the National Fatherhood Initiative, an organization that has been remarkably successful in promoting the idea of responsible fatherhood. It has started state organizations that sponsor fatherhood programs and has brought the issue of fatherlessness and its consequences to the attention of both federal and state legislatures. The Ford Foundation, under the leadership of Ron Mincy, has committed energy, leadership, and resources to finding flexible new strategies for promoting fatherhood among low-income groups. Remarkable grass roots programs such as Joe Jones's Center for Fathers, Families, and Work Force Development and Charles Ballard's Institute for Responsible Fatherhood have specialized in promoting fatherhood among poor, generally black, inner-city communities. Although there are differences between these two programs, they both identify young men who are fathers, try to relate them to their newborn infants, explain the needs of these children and their mothers, and model risk-free adult male behavior. These young men, it is reported, are often proud to be fathers, interested in their children, and open to learning how to relate to their offspring more positively. Avance has found that CBOs can also be useful in helping fathers find jobs, become better parents, gain needed community support, and establish a social support network.

As a result of this combination of basic research and practical programs, new studies of practical intervention with young fathers and their families is now proceeding. Most notable among these is the Fragile Families and Child Wellbeing Study directed by Irwin Garfunkel and Sara McLanahan.[74] This investigation is studying low-income fathers, especially unmarried fathers, to determine their situation, their attitudes toward government efforts to enforce child support payments, and their views about their children and their children's mothers. The attitudes of mothers also are being studied. All of this is designed to find ways to promote more cooperation between unmarried parents with an eye toward improving the well-being of their children, especially during the first three years of life. Much of this research is stimulated by a fear that increasingly tough child support payments imposed by government on fathers are unrealistic for the poorest of them. Indeed, these enforcement programs may function to further alienate fathers from their families or put them in jail rather than helping them move into more cooperative and responsible relationships with their children and their children's mother. There is a strong motivation in the fragile families study to learn how to help poor fathers do both—take steps toward meeting financial obligations to their children but also to relate to their offspring in more positive and supportive ways.

Ron Mincy of the Ford Foundation believes this research will help design ways of enhancing communication and problem solving between unmarried parents. Aspects of the communication education movement described in the first part of this chapter may prove relevant even to unmarried, low-income, low-education parents. It will be surprising, however, if the marriage education movement, developed mainly for middle-class couples, can become relevant to the diversity of low-income groups without considerable revision. It is plausible to believe, however, that all people can learn these skills when properly taught. In short, there must be not only more jobs for low-income males, better welfare supports, better job training, literacy programs, and a more favorable tax environment (in short, a whole range of social systemic interventions), but society also must create a new culture of parenting and the educational supports aimed at specific persons to help them develop new attitudes, motivations, and skills. So far, the issue of how to address the emerging culture of nonmarriage, and the weakening of parenting that this nearly always entails, has not been addressed adequately by anybody, with the possible exception of some African American churches. Communicative skills and social reinforcements will not be enough to reconstitute and reformulate the institutions of marriage and family; this will require, as we have argued time and again, a huge intellectual and coordinated cultural work and a new public philosophy and policy for these institutions.

The goals of better communication and higher levels of cooperation between nonresidential parents do not preclude movement by such couples toward marriage. Although there is a debate in the fatherhood movement about just how central marriage ought to be, especially among groups where it has drastically declined and nonmarital births are high, there is growing acceptance of the idea that a marriage movement in these quarters should be encouraged by both government and the institutions of civil society. This is one of the many goals of the bill called Fathers Count introduced in the House of Representatives and a similar bipartisan bill introduced by Pete Dominici and Evan Bayh in the U.S. Senate. Although neither bill tries to mandate or enforce marriage, both believe that government can be supportive by telling the story about the functional goods of marriage and by making sure that the state does not develop laws and programs that accidentally discourage it.

Implicit in these new bills and the fragile families study is a distinction between *prevention* and *intervention*. For unmarried couples who have had children and also still have some tentative or "fragile" contact with one another, good intervention entails education for better communication and parenting. Marriage often cannot be the first goal; either the father or mother may have married or may be presently cohabiting with another partner. Marriage may not be a possibility, but better communication and parenting are possibilities. However, for the long-term future of communities where marriage deinstitutionalization is advanced, prevention may be in order. This means both creating a new culture of marriage and helping couples in love take concrete steps toward marriage *before* having their first child. Building a new marriage climate in communities where the institution has fallen into disfavor is a work that first should be stimulated by local community organizations and churches. Such work can then properly become a goal of government programs. And finally, building a marriage culture should be a responsibility of market forces that all too often entice troubled families with destructive styles of consumption at the same time that they may deprive such families of the benefits of a living wage.

A good direction and the right balance can be found in a recent statement titled "Turning the Corner on Father Absence in Black America" (1999) released by the Morehouse Research Institute and the Institute for American Values. This statement—signed by leading figures in the black community such as Elijah Anderson, Stephen Carter, Glenn Loury, Ronald Mincy, and William Julius Wilson—acknowledges that the situation of black men has been created by both cultural factors such as racism and individualism *and* social systemic factors such as joblessness, low salaries, poor schools, and exclusion from the digital revolution. Since both cultural and social systemic factors place great psychological stress on black men—and, as Orlando Patterson (1998) argues, have done so since the days of slavery—the cure must also be both cultural *and* social systemic. The signers of the Morehouse statement write:

Although we differ on the relative weight to be given to economic, cultural, and private and public policy factors in shaping the lives of African American fathers, we agree that each of these factors is at work, and that comprehensive strategies are needed to confront the crisis of father absence in the African American community. Although we differ on how to enhance marriage, we do agree that a key goal of the fatherhood movement must be to encourage both enhanced marriageability *and* healthy marriages.

The report acknowledges the need for fairer economic opportunities for African American fathers. But it also points to a profound "spiritual dimension" in the fatherhood crisis, the need for a new marriage culture, and the importance of churches and community organizations in creating this new culture. It calls for better marriage and parenting education, but, more broadly, it calls for better schools and teachers across the board. In short, this statement illustrates the kind of complex strategy that we have argued for time and again in this book—cultural reconstruction, social systemic change, and concrete educational work with individuals.

Mothers and Children

Mothers must be treated as persons. They should not be seen solely from the perspective of abstract maternal cultural symbols, nor should they be reduced to the roles and expectations of our social systems. This is why the research of the Fragile Families and Child Wellbeing Study is right to study the attitudes and perspectives of mothers as well as fathers. This is why Charles Ballard, Joe Jones, and Ron Mincy are correct in wanting to work with both fathers and mothers around communication issues, even if they are not married. Every strategy of intervention must keep the individual mother in mind. Workfare must keep the tremendous individual struggles of the working mother in mind—her health needs, her education needs, her child care needs, and her community support needs. *The entire field of relationship education has potential for helping with the myriad of communication problems that families of all forms face, especially the challenges of single mothers.*
The field of parent education is still underdeveloped for

all families, but especially for pressured single mothers. One of the most successful features of the work of Avance, the family service program for Hispanics described in chapter 6, is its work in parent education. This is the key to the bilingual and bicultural education that we have called for in this book. The best negotiation of the forces of modernity comes from those communities with sufficient cultural cohesion to retrieve and build on settled wisdom even as they adapt to the more positive aspects of the modernizing process. Parent education should center precisely on this task and help mothers and fathers address a wide range of issues confronting families on the borderline between tradition and modernity. This includes issues in the area of cognitive learning, the early brain stimulation of infants, moral education, sex education, and training in emerging modern technologies. It is possible that the entire field of sex education should be reconceived as parent education to help mothers and fathers handle the tensions between tradition and modernization in the field of sexual conduct. Most of the insights from the field of communication education also apply to the field of parenting. Indeed, much of the parenting literature has been written by people who also have written for the area of communication education in the fields of marriage and family.

Mothers and fathers need support—especially poor single parents, parents with special needs children, and parents in the military. Counseling and mental health services can be of vital importance to families dealing with abuse, be it physical, mental, or substance abuse. Schools, churches, and community centers can be seen as family support centers where parents come together to receive needed services and strengthen their social support network.

To keep mothers in mind, we must review public programs for families not only from the perspective of mothers in the wage economy but also of mothers who spend their time mainly in domestic chores and child care. Present tax breaks covering costs of professional child care must be balanced with equal tax help for families where one parent stays home while the other is the primary breadwinner. Although we have recommended the sixty-hour work week as a model for those families where both husband and wife work in the wage economy, culture and society must stop short of presenting this model as a universal expectation. Some families, for a variety of reasons, will elect to have only one breadwinner, and it is likely that the majority of parents choosing not to work in the wage economy will continue to be wives and mothers. Society cannot allow itself to be uncritically market dominated, i.e., it must not push families to become totally embedded in the logics and demands of the wage economy. The market should not become an all-consuming reality for families. Nor should society become unwittingly prejudicial against families with only one breadwinner, even as it tries to support the majority of families presently electing for both parents to gain outside incomes. Furthermore, the sixty-hour work week as a maximum for a husband-wife team has implications for workfare. Single parents forced to find employment must be able to find thirty-hour positions that leave some remaining time and energy for the tremendous responsibilities of parenthood.

9

Notes on Some
Very Hard Questions

Family is a huge topic. Add the subject of marriage to it, and it gets larger still. Think of how many matters we have touched on so far—culture, religion, the state, civil society, taxes, welfare, the professions, marriage education, fatherhood, motherhood, children, and many more. We are embarrassed to have addressed so many issues—not an elegant thing to do in this era of specialization. You ask and we ask—where is the end? No wonder that our society is confused about family: it is simply too big a topic for our little brains. Family is at the nexus of a vast number of cultural and social forces; touch the subject of family and you get involved in an endless number of other areas. And that alone may be the reason why families are so important.

And yet there are additional areas that we should address. These are the really hard questions—the ones readers doubtless often wondered about as they read the foregoing pages. All the issues we have discussed are hard ones, but some family issues are especially difficult because they so deeply arouse our emotions. *These are the issues of teenage pregnancies, sex education, domestic violence, the media, homosexual marriage, and abortion.* These are all subjects that in some way pertain to the family. These topics have at times been explosive in our society. In fact, they have sometimes so dominated discussions about the family that other central issues have been pushed off the table and out of social awareness. This book, on the other hand, has worked the other way. We have struggled in these pages to bring back into public consciousness many of the issues that have been obscured by the dominance of these so-called hot-button issues. We have tried to state an approach that might create some rough consensus about these issues. We hope that if we have made progress on these matters that the very hard questions can be more fruitfully addressed.

Health, Marriage, and the Hard Questions

We have made the promotion of good marriages—more specifically, equal regard marriages—a fairly central strategy, although not the only strategy, for addressing the growing family disruption of our society. We have tried to weave a tapestry of contributions from government, civil society, and market. We know that in making these proposals, we are flying in the face of massive social and cultural forces associated with the modernization process. We know that many prominent social scientists believe we are foolhardy to think that the tide of these forces can be turned. But we do not believe these social forces are inevitable. Just as many people today are trying to halt the destruction of the natural environment through the ecological movement, we should with equal fervor try to halt the disruption of the family and its web of supporting institutions. In fact, family should be an extension of our ecological concerns.

In many ways, all of these issues can be seen as conflicts between certain contemporary models of health and normative traditions of marriage and family inherited from the past. Health versus tradition: do the contemporary controversies on issues of sex and family really come down to that? Well, almost. That formula is a little too simplistic, but it does shed considerable light on present disputes. *The conflict underlying many of these issues is an individualistic understanding of mental and physical health that is disconnected from questions about the public good and disassociated from certain religiocultural institutions—institutions designed to contribute to human flourishing by organizing conflicting goods in ways that enhance, channel, and sometimes limit individual fulfillment.*

Teenage Pregnancies and Sex Education

We will discuss together the areas of sex education, teenage pregnancy, and sexually transmitted diseases (STDs). According to the National Campaign to Prevent Teenage Pregnancy, nonmarital births to teen girls constitute one of the most significant disruptions to family and marriage lurking in contemporary society. The goal of sex education courses (today mainly referred to as "comprehensive sex education") is to reduce among teens unwanted pregnancies and sexually transmitted diseases. Both of these goals are health goals. Teenage pregnancies and nonmarital births contribute, as we have seen above, to the poverty of women and children, to stress of various kinds, to higher rates of abuse between mother and infant, and to higher rates of difficulties later in school, employment, and family formation for the children. All of these declines add up to poorer mental and physical health. In addition, the sexual activity that led to the teenage pregnancy may have given rise to STDs that can damage the health, or even end the lives, of both the young mother and her offspring. So obviously, in the name of mental and physical health, society should do everything it can to reduce disease and early pregnancy. But how?

One of the big answers has emphasized education that acquaints students with reproductive information and methods of safe sex—sex that does not lead to unwanted pregnancies and disease. Comprehensive sex education adds insights into uncoerced decision making and concern and respect for both self and other. What is missing in these curricula is the word marriage—its place in sexuality and, more than anything, its health benefits. Even the well-respected curriculum prepared by Dr. Marian Howard of Emory University Medical School emphasizes the delay of sexuality, saying little about marriage as such.[75]

Now, there are good reasons for this disassociation of sexual activity and marriage in these educational approaches; they assume that many young people have already disconnected sex and marriage, at least in their teenage and young adult years. Since that has happened and could well continue to happen, the reasoning goes that in the name of health, alternative means of protection from pregnancy and disease should be provided. Hence, sex education in public schools has, for the most part, reflected what was thought to be happening in society; since sexual activity more and more is being freed from marriage, sex education must reflect this disconnection in order to promote healthy sexuality. And this must be done even if sex education as such goes against the sexual philosophies of all the classic religiocultural traditions that have shaped our society's historic sensibilities about the organization of sexuality in human life. In fact, a recent review issued by the Park Ridge Center of the positions of all the major faith traditions—Protestant (liberal and conservative), Catholic, Jewish, Buddhist, and Islam—demonstrates that historically all have emphasized refraining from sexual activity until marriage.[76] Even Buddhism, which is the most secular of the world religions in its view of marriage, has been cautious about adolescent sexuality. Liberal Protestant groups such as the Episcopalians are conservative on this issue. The United Church of Christ and the Unitarian/Universalists may be the exceptions.

So, here is the dilemma: should the health establishment have the upper hand in teaching sexual health to young people or should our various religiocultural traditions take the lead? We feel that this is a genuinely difficult question. Sexual practices have changed. Youth pay less attention to their parents' traditions. These traditions themselves have less influence on their followers. Furthermore, these traditions have shown little appetite for actually effectively teaching their traditions. And finally, the U.S. has a policy of separation between religion and the state; therefore, should these traditions have the right to dictate health policies for all?

Of course, the answer is "no"; they should not, individually or collectively, dictate health policy for our nation's youth. But they should not be ignored. Public policy has every right to be primarily concerned about basic health. *But it should not promote health values at the expense of undercutting important religiocultural traditions, especially if these traditions themselves are productive of health for those who truly follow their teachings. Ironically, the research into the benefits of marriage and the negative consequences of divorce and nonmarital births demonstrates that the institution of marriage on the whole does promote health. Hence, in the name of health, sex education in our society should become even more comprehensive. It should educate young people into the health values of marriage. It should help youth begin developing the skills for good relationships and marriages, and these should be even more important than the skills needed to avoid pregnancy and disease. And good sex education should help students appreciate the wisdom of communities of commitment so that the language of health is not the only language ordering the field of sexuality, family, and marriage.* To make these general points should not lead the reader to forget that time and again in this book we have admitted that religious and cultural traditions often need criticism. We also have argued that this can best be done through deeper understanding of these traditions and the ways in which resources for the reformulation of their practices can often be found within the traditions themselves.

Of course, there are many more issues to be discussed in the domain of sex education that go beyond the scope of our book. Our main point is this: increasingly the sex education movement and the marriage education movement should come together. It might even be better if the three fields of sex education, marriage education, and parent education would come together. Gloria Rodriguez's extensive experience in parent education leads her to believe that parents themselves may be the best people to negotiate the treacherous waters between health values, morality, marriage education, and tradition. And it may well be that the center of concentration in the future for any cooperation between these three educational fields might be in a setting that made parents at the center. It is too early to anticipate all the difficult issues involved in forming a closer relation between these three movements, but it will be a happy revolution for all of them, we believe, if they move into closer relation with one another.

Domestic Violence

Our position has implications for the phenomenon of domestic violence. This is a serious issue in our society. Our argument for the importance of marriage for strong families and healthy children should not be misunderstood; we are not arguing for marriage at any cost. We are not saying couples should remain married in face of persistent violence, drug and alcohol abuse, and other kinds of dangerous activities. We believe that many difficulties that have led to divorce over the last four decades can be resolved with better preparation, intervention, and a host of other supports, but we are aware that not all conflicts can and should avoid legal separation. And although marriage contributes to economic well-being for couples and to better school and job performance for children—thereby helping to close the income gap—society must not be insensitive to the reality of spousal and child abuse of various kinds.

But there is much misleading information abroad about the major source of domestic violence and abuse. If one reads the popular press, and a good deal of social science scholarship, one might conclude that marriage is a "hitting license" for violent husbands to abuse their wives and children. This impression arises from a simple yet profound confusion that runs throughout these reports—the tendency to blur the distinction between marriage and other kinds of living arrangements such as cohabitation, dating, and various kinds of informal sexual relationships. In their recent exhaustive review of the scientific evidence for the health benefits of marriage in *The Case for Marriage* (2000), Linda Waite and Maggie Gallagher write, "Domestic violence is perhaps the only area in which social scientists casually use the term *husband* to mean any or all of the following: the man one is married to, the man one used to be married to, the man one lives with, the man one is merely having sex with, and/or the man one used to have sex with." When these distinctions are made, presently married husbands are proportionately far less violent than men in other relationships. As Waite and Gallagher pithily put it, "But the research clearly shows that, outside of hying thee to a nunnery, the safest place for a woman to be is inside marriage."

A few facts from *The Case for Marriage* will give reality to this statement. Wives are far less likely to be crime victims than single women; when all crimes are considered, single and divorced women are four to five times more likely to be victims. Single and divorced women were almost ten times more likely to be victims of rape and three times more likely to be victims of aggravated assault than wives. Marriage protects men as well; bachelors are four times more likely to be objects of violence than husbands. Only 8 percent of wives and 6 percent of husbands in a 1994 survey reported that any of their arguments had become physical in the past year. Of this group, 18 percent of wives and 7 percent of their husbands were cut, bruised, or seriously injured. The National Crime Victimization Survey conducted by the U.S. Department of Justice reported that of all violent crimes against partners that occurred between 1979 and 1987, 65 percent were committed by boyfriends or ex-husbands. Husbands presently living with their wives committed 9 percent of these crimes. A redesigned study changed the statistics somewhat; 55 percent were committed by boyfriends, 31 percent by husbands, and 14 percent by ex-husbands.[77] Waite and Gallagher speculate that the two reasons boyfriends and cohabitors are more prone to violence are that the couple is less committed to each other and more isolated from other social networks and controls.

Good marriages will also reduce violence between parents and children. The physical and sexual abuse of children is much higher in cohabiting families and step families. Boyfriends and stepfathers are far more likely to abuse the children of their girl friends than married husbands and biologically related fathers. Evolutionary psychologists believe kin altruism alone, stemming from the genetic relatedness of biological parents to their children, functions to inhibit violence by a parent against his or her own flesh and blood.[78] Sociologists also hypothesize that the larger number of social controls organized around marriage as a legal and public institution further function to inhibit parental violence against their children. Both reasons may have a degree of validity.

It seems to follow that whatever produces better marriages is likely to reduce domestic violence. But, of course, not just any marriage will do. It must be an equal regard marriage with good communication, good community supports, and one without overwhelming pressures from finances and work. Hence, in addition to good law enforcement and zero tolerance of all forms of domestic violence, including violence between husband and wife, good marital preparation, good conflict resolution skills, good jobs, and good tax supports for overstressed parents should go far to lower domestic violence for present and future generations.

Health, Reproductive Technology, and the Traditions

Much of what we have said about sex education has significance for the entire field of reproductive technology. When surveying this arena of medicine, we are struck by its speed of change, its unregulated status, and its market driven features. This entire area is a marvelous example of how technical rationality as science and technical rationality as market conspire together to shape the life world of intimate relations in family and marriage. We have the utmost sympathy for married couples who face reproductive problems, and we both are deeply grateful for the breakthroughs of modern medicine that make it possible for countless couples who otherwise might never achieve this goal to conceive and have children.

But we are struck by an emerging cultural contradiction. At the same time that there is a visible and increasingly powerful movement to both encourage and reformulate marriage in our society, the field of reproductive technology seems more or less absent from these discussions. Throughout the country individuals and couples, regardless of marital status, are being credited with reproductive rights and often, even with public financing, given assistance in having a child.[79] Our point is simple: isn't it time to have a careful culture-wide discussion as to whether marriage itself is one of the preconditions for being qualified to use reproductive assistance in having a child? Doesn't it seem to suggest that marriage is only incidental and basically unimportant to child rearing to grant this privilege to those who have not gone through the publicly sanctioned preparations and registrations that marriage entails? *If increasingly we recommend, or sometimes even require, high school students, college students, and engaged couples to become educated for marriage and parenting, isn't it strange not to ask individuals and couples who use reproductive technology to have this education and, finally, the public marital status itself?* One might counter that many singles have children out-of-wedlock and vast numbers of cohabiting couples do as well. Society does not, and should not, criminalize this activity or otherwise take coercive steps to restrict it. So, what is the problem? Shouldn't singles and unmarried couples have the benefits of reproductive technology as well? At this point, we are making no strong recommendations about the legal restriction of reproductive assistance for the unmarried. But we are asking for a cultural discussion and a new sensibility among health professionals that reconsider the relation of reproductive technology to marriage.

Gay Families, Gay Marriage

In chapter 7 we took our most controversial stance. There we advanced the position of discouraging the extension of what legal scholar Carl Schneider calls "marriage equivalents." This means we view the extension of marriage-like privileges through the institution of domestic partnership as a threat to the institution of marriage itself. We believe that marriage is in the best interest of both individuals and the common good; marriage, as we have argued, provides a wide range of freely elected protections and accountabilities—protections and accountabilities that the state is increasingly finding it necessary to impose on unmarried cohabitors without their free agreement and consent. It is doing this for understandable reasons—to solve conflicts over children, money, property, and other damages. So, as the reader knows well by now, we are high on marriage and low on marital equivalents.

But what does this mean for marriage between homosexuals? Since domestic partnerships are widely used to grant marriage-like privileges and protections to these couples, what would a social withdrawal from this institution mean for them? Would gay and lesbian couples need to turn to the institution of marriage or would they need to rehabilitate the concept of friendship, live without these protections, or gain them through the mechanism of individually negotiated legal contracts and other procedures?

As we indicated early in the book, we will take no stand on this issue. We shy away from the burden of such a stand because of its complex scholarly entailments. It is not an easy question. There are reasons to move away from marital equivalents. But is homosexual marriage a good idea? We feel we can be of most service by summarizing the arguments to the best of our ability—better, we hope, than is often done.

Here are the arguments for homosexual marriage. First, many homosexual couples are in love with each other in ways that mirror current grounds for marriage among heterosexuals. This love gets to the core of their identities as human beings. Therefore, it is unjust to deny them the institution of marriage. Second, homosexual relations between couples in love need protections (insurance, visitation rights when ill, ways of settling disputes) and formal marriage affords these protections. Third, religiocultural and associated legal traditions that have forbidden homosexual marriage are more complicated than they appear at first glance and may not necessarily oppose such unions when more carefully interpreted. And fourth, marriage has a stabilizing effect on loving relationships; homosexual relations, especially among males, need the settling influence of the formal institution of marriage.

The arguments against extending marriage to gays and lesbians are quite parallel. First, some say that to extend marital privileges and responsibilities to homosexual couples is inherently unjust; it discriminates against nonerotic friendships and groups sharing economies of scale who might also want these privileges and protections. But to extend these privileges and protections so broadly throughout society is unworkable and finally renders marriage meaningless. Second, the protections of marriage as an institution are largely associated with its childbearing and rearing aspects. Although marriage includes strong affectional dimensions that are becoming even more prominent, the institution of marriage *qua* institution must not be reduced to these features but should also be connected with the needs and demands of procreation and child care. Third, all the axial religiocultural traditions have discouraged homosexuality, with the possible exception of Buddhism, and none has advocated homosexual marriage. Fourth, absent the interests of what marital stability means for children, there is little special state interest in the stability of homosexual relations and little evidence that the institution of marriage alone, without its primary childbearing and rearing functions, would have these stabilizing effects.

Each of these arguments can be expanded and nuanced. Each can be answered, at least preliminarily. The debate can and will go on and on and become quite complex before it is finally resolved. The direction of countries such as France where marriage-like benefits have been extended to all kinds of couples, and not just heterosexual or homosexual love relationships, testifies to both the confusions and possible directions of the current debate. However it is finally resolved, we maintain our view that the spread of the concept of domestic partnerships as a legal category is an unfavorable development for both society and the institution of marriage.

The Media

No book on the family can fail to mention the power of the media to affect family relationships. The role of the media, however, in producing family disruption should neither be overestimated or underestimated. We have argued that there are many sources of marital disruption, mostly stemming from the interaction of cultural individualism and technical rationality. The media—movies and television— are just special arenas of social action, among many, in which this interaction takes place. The formula goes like this: individualistic and unregulated expressions of sexual activity (individualism) sell (market values), and the powerful media of movies and television (examples of technical rationality) can be used to accomplish this alliance between cultural and market values. The result? An uncritical glamorization and normalization of nonmarital sexual and romantic relationships that is especially misleading to the young.

The cure is difficult to develop and implement. For good reasons, artistic censorship that is legally enforced is neither consistent with American values nor effective. The two of us can only recommend vigorous, free, and open cultural criticism occasionally coupled with market retaliations against advertisers who consistently sponsor programing that is disruptive and insulting to family and marital stability. Distinctions must always be made between pro-

grams that investigate mature issues in love and family relations; after all, we do not live in a perfect world, and we must
be able to investigate artistically human mistakes as well as
virtues, the ambiguities of life as well as its more elevated expressions. But this level of artistry can be distinguished from
intentional and habitual exploitations that are misleading to
the young and damaging in general to the human spirit.

The most promising avenue of action is found in those
voluntary organizations that monitor the media and disseminate their research. We are especially impressed with work
of the Parents Television Council, The National Institute on
Media and the Family, and the critical review of cinema by
Los Angeles Archbishop Roger Cardinal Mahony. There
needs to be even more of this kind of activity.

The Last Hard Question: Abortion

As we indicated at the beginning of the book, we will not
try to solve the question of abortion, as important as it is. Instead, we will try to glean some lessons from the national experience of debating that difficult issue. We must continue
to discuss in a civil way this important matter and not simply
exhaust our energies trying to win legislative and legal victo-
ries through the display of political power and legal maneu-
ver. But it is possible to improve our conversations—to make
them less like wars and more like dialogues. First, it is important to respect the views of both sides of this debate. There
are good reasons for both points of view. Those who want to
protect the right to have an abortion realize that women
bear the greater risks in childbirth and that their health and
well-being are often threatened by pregnancy. Furthermore,
children should come into the world wanted and loved, not
resented or possibly even rejected. It is also true, however,
that it is difficult to determine if or when a fetus is a human
being. Furthermore, the right of a man to decide whether or
not to become a father needs to be respected more than is
presently the case. The abortion debate is no place for one
or the other side to believe that it has all the truth.

Second, more than any other debate over family matters presently occurring in our society, the abortion issue begs for an ethics of discourse. Jürgen Habermas advances several features of a discourse ethic that we believe are relevant for talking not only about the abortion issue but also all the hard topics discussed in this chapter. According to him, in all discourse or dialogue one must be willing to make empirical assertions with credibility, acknowledge the norms governing one's speech, and speak with honesty and authenticity.[80] Deeper than that, Habermas believes that all good or "ideal" speech situations entail a permission for all participants to speak, a respect for and solidarity with the dialogue partner, and a renunciation of force and deceit.[81] There is, as we have pointed out above, considerable continuity between a discourse ethic between couples in the marital or premarital situation and the discourse ethic our society needs to develop a viable public philosophy and public policy governing issues pertaining to family and marriage.

Our final thought is this: we live during a time when Americans desperately need to learn the ethics of discourse for both situations—the family context itself and the public square where our family philosophies and policies will be established. It is through such discourse that we will weave the tapestry that will revitalize family and marriage. It is, as we have argued, a complex work of culture.

Summary of Recommendations

General Principles

1. Consensus on family issues comes best when conflicting cultural and religious traditions are taken seriously and interpreted and analogies between them discovered and developed.

2. The social sciences cannot directly be a foundation for family policy, but they can refine and help critique conflicting values in inherited family traditions.

3. These traditions contribute an important range of in-

trinsic values that help resist the increasingly utilitarian and cost-benefit language that is now widely used in the social sciences and society to understand, and sometimes justify, family and marriage. In short, they contribute various languages of commitment.

4. A critical marriage culture is crucial for the overall health of families.

5. Marriage is a multidimensional institution that historically has been seen to have natural, contractual, social, and religious dimensions. For the last 400 years one of the members of the marriage contract has been the state, making marriage in part a public institution. This should be retained.

Family, Marriage, and Civil Society

1. The renewal of marriage and family is first a task of civil society, with government and market playing important but subordinate roles.

2. Religious institutions make up a major part of civil society, at least in the United States. The Common Marriage Policy of the Roman Catholic Church and the emerging ecumenical Community Marriage Policy should be encouraged, systematically evaluated, and possibly extended to new local communities.

3. The Community Marriage Policy, now confined primarily to religious institutions, should be extended to entire communities and include all sectors and professions relevant to marriage and family. Since these programs already have begun to develop, these initiatives need evaluation.

4. Many of the initiatives addressing marriage and family issues should also emerge from community based organizations—often funded in part by public money—that are close to the traditions and culture of those they serve.

5. Professions serving families at the community level—law, ministry, education, psychotherapy, medicine, etc.— should become more aware of the new research showing the health benefits of marriage and take appropriate steps toward being supportive of marriage within the boundaries of good professional practice.

Family, Marriage, and Government

1. Government policies pertaining to family and marriage should grow out of the free discourse of civil society as this influences the legislative process.

2. The welfare reforms of 1996 emphasizing movement of the poor into paid employment can only function successfully if working parents receive essential supports such as medical insurance, help with day care for children, help with transportation, education and job training, assistance in finding jobs, and food stamps.

3. TANF funds should be used for marriage education, but first of all on programs that actually reach the poor.

4. Cooperation between government and CBOs in supporting families and marriage should be encouraged as long as church-state and charitable-choice guidelines are respected.

5. Marriage penalties—both those connected with the transition from welfare to self-sufficiency and those associated with increased taxation due to the higher tax brackets of dual income marriages—should be removed.

6. Some family supports applying specifically to children should be universal and given to all families with children, regardless of form or marital status. These include our proposed increases in tax credits (from $500 to $1,000 or perhaps $1,500) dependent deductions (from $2,750 to possibly $8,200), and a new Dependent Care Tax reduction to all parents of $700–$800 per child regardless of whether professional child care is used.

7. Caution should be exercised in the creation of legal functional equivalents to marriage.

8. Covenant marriage laws, super-vows, and children-first divorce reform should be studied and possibly extended.

9. Governments should enforce zero tolerance laws against domestic violence. But they should also realize that steps that improve marriage also will decrease both spousal and child abuse.

10. Since good marriages contribute to lowering the income gap, governments should acknowledge this reality and institute various pro-marriage initiatives in an effort to help the poor.

Family, Marriage, and Market

1. Government should encourage, and sometimes require, business to pay family wages, provide basic health insurance, and give sufficient medical and family leaves at levels consistent with basic human needs and special obligations to family members.

2. The market should investigate the concept of the sixty-hour week in paid employment for couples with children and take steps to provide the part-time jobs, flexible working arrangements, child care, and basic health care packages consistent with the institutionalization and extension of this model of employment.

Persons

1. The marriage education movement is maturing and becoming better grounded in research and delivery. It should be extended to religious institutions, high schools and colleges, and businesses.

2. Marriage education should be supported by government in accordance with historic understandings of marriage

as simultaneously a public, personal, and sacred institution.

3. Fathers are important for families and children, and civil society, market, and government should encourage and support marriage for fathers; but they should also support fathers contributing and caring for their children when marriage is impossible.

4. Parent education is relevant for all families, regardless of form, and increasingly should be investigated as the best context, although not the only context, for enhancing early childhood cognitive, moral, emotional, and sexual development and education. Civil society, government, and market should cooperate in promoting parent education.

Notes

1 Rodriguez (1999); Browning et al. (2000).
2 Witte (1997).
3 Amitai Etzioni, "A Nation of Minorities?" *The Responsive Community?* (Winter 1999/2000), p. 13.
4 This is often called the "naturalistic fallacy," a term contributed to modern philosophy by the British philosopher G.E. Moore (1965).
5 Bernstein (1983).
6 For a discussion of how a narrow empiricism can function in ways to alienate us from our cultural heritage, see Ricouer (1981), pp. 64–65.
7 Winch (1958); Gadamer (1982); Ricoeur (1974); Bernstein (1983), pp. 8–9; Rorty (1979); Derrida (1973).
8 Witte (1997), pp. 42–73, 37–39.
9 We will be following Hans-Georg Gadamer by looking within traditions for the classics that have shaped the ideals of particular traditions. We will differ from Gadamer in holding that classics also can be critiqued as well as understood. See Gadamer (1982), pp. 255–258.
10 For the classic statement on the economic analysis of the family, see Becker (1991).

11   Carey Goldberg, "Hispanic Households Struggle As Incomes Decline," *The New York Times* (January 30, 1997, p. 1-A).

12   There are various contemporary understandings of the role of critique in modern life. We follow those views held by Bernstein and Ricoeur that locate critique of tradition within a prior attempt to appreciate and understand it. See Bernstein (1983), pp. 154–155; and Ricoeur (1981), pp. 77–87.

13   For a position that believes justice is a modern invention and cannot be found in the traditions, see Okin (1999).

14   Trible (1978), p. 18. After close textual analysis of the logic of the metaphors involved in the words "When God created humankind, in the likeness of God made he him; male and female created he them," Trible writes, "The parallelism between . . . 'male and female' shows further that sexual differentiation does not mean hierarchy but rather equality."

15   "The Marriage Movement" (New York: The Institute for American Values, 2000). This statement was jointly issued by the Institute for American Values, The Coalition of Marriage, Family, and Couples Education, and the Religion, Culture, and Family Project of the University of Chicago and signed by a diverse group of liberal and conservative family-policy leaders.

16   Steven Nock, "The Problem with Marriage," *Society* (July/August 1999), pp. 150–154; and Nock (1998), pp. 130–140.

17   Browning et al. (2000), p. 19.

18   Weber (1958), pp. 181–182.

19   Goode (1993), p. 13.

20   For statements of this point of view, see Reed (1994); Reed (1996); and Dobson and Bauer (1990).

21   For a comprehensive review of these mixtures, see Brundage (1987).

22   Richard Posner (1992), p. 192, minimizes the importance of fathers if economic resources can otherwise be secured.

23   George W. Brown, M.N. Bhrolchain, and T. Harris, "Social Class and Psychiatric Disorders in Women in Urban Populations," *Sociology* 9 (1975), pp. 225–254; P. Miller and J.G. Ingham, "Friends, Confidants, and Symptoms," *Social Psychiatry* 11 (1976), pp. 51–58.

24   Amato (1998), pp. 241–278; Popenoe (1996), pp. 139–163; Snarey (1993); McLanahan and Sandefur (1994), pp. 18–38.

25   For a helpful summary of this debate, see Eric Bryant Rhodes, "Fatherhood Matters," *The American Prospect* (March 13, 2000), pp. 48–52.

26 Nock (1998), pp. 74–80.

27 John Laub, Daniel Nagin, and Robert Sampson, "Trajectories of Change in Criminal Offending: Good Marriage and the Desistance Process," *American Sociological Review* 63:2 (April 1998), pp. 225–238.

28 Nock (1998), pp. 74–83.

29 Ronald Simons, Kueli-Hsiu Lin, Leslie Gordon, Rand Conger, and Frederick Lorenz, "Explaining the Higher Incidence of Adjustment Problems Among Children of Divorce Compared with Those in Two-Parent Families," *Journal of Marriage and Family* 61 (November 1999), pp. 1020–1034.

30 The higher figure was advanced by Weitzman (1985). The lower figure was given by Furstenberg and Cherlin (1992), p. 50.

31 Schneider (1996), p. 192.

32 *Marriage in America: A Report to the Nation.* (New York: Institute for American Values, 1995).

33 Browning et al. (2000), pp. 272–305.

34 Smith (1999), p. 1.

35 Linda Waite, "The Negative Effects of Cohabitation," *The Responsive Community* (Winter 2000), p. 31. Also see Waite and Gallagher (2000), pp. 36–46.

36 *Ibid.* See also, Popenoe and Whitehead (1999).

37 The field of evolutionary psychology, using the same theories of kin altruism and inclusive fitness, sometimes paints humans as quite egoistic but at other times as quite empathic and generous. For the first point of view, see Dawkins (1976), and for the second point of view, see De Waal (1996). Modern theology could accept both views but would add that the real root of human evil is a result of anxiety and the misuse of freedom that end in compounding these conflicting tendencies. See Niebuhr (1941), pp. 181–184.

38 Shorter (1975), p. 21; Stone (1990), p. 391.

39 For a sample of this point of view, see Furstenburg and Cherlin (1992), pp. 99–106.

40 Habermas (1977), pp. 340–365; Wolfe (1989), p. 20.

41 Ron Lesthaege, "A Century of Demographic and Cultural Change in Western Europe," *Population and Development Review* 9:3 (September 1983), pp. 411–432.

42 For an excellent historical account of this process, see Ryan (1981).

43 Engels (1972), pp. 134–140.

44 Becker (1991), p. 356.

45 Okin (1989).

46 Herbert Marcuse caught this insight into Freud when he pointed out that the "reality principle," to which Freud thought every healthy ego should conform, was actually captured by bourgeois industrialism, hence Freud's unwitting definition of mental health in ways that put it into the service of the modernization process. See Marcuse (1955), pp. 78–105.

47 Witte (1997), pp. 42–73.

48 Witte (1997), pp. 25–23; Brundage (1987), pp. 264–265.

49 Brundage (1987), pp. 189–190, 276–278; Ozment (1983), pp. 29–31.

50 For an analysis of how conceptual thought, even scientific concepts, rests on a sea of deep metaphors, see Lakoff and Johnson (1980). For an analysis of how the social sciences rest on such metaphors, see Browning (1987).

51 Browning (1987), pp. 32–60, 94–116, 161–203, 204–238.

52 Peter Donovan, "Do Different Religions Share Moral Common Ground?" *Religious Studies* 22 (September-December 1986), pp. 31–55; Raimundo Panikkar, "Is the Notion of Human Rights a Western Concept?" *Diogenes* 120 (Winter 1982), pp. 75–102.

53 McManus (1993), pp. 293–318.

54 Markman, Stanley, and Blumberg (1994); Stanley, Trathern, McCain, and Bryan (1998).

55 Vaughn Call and Tim Heaton, "Religious Influence on Marital Stability," *Journal for the Scientific Study of Religion* 36 (1997), pp. 382–392.

56 Larry Bumpass and James Sweet, "Cohabitation, Marriage and Union Stability," NSFH Working Paper No. 65. Madison: University of Wisconsin, Center for Demography and Ecology, 1991.

57 Christopher Ellison, John Bartkowski, and Kristin Anderson, "Are There Religious Variations in Domestic Violence?" *Journal of Family Issues* 20 (1999), pp. 87–113.

58 William Doherty, "How Therapists Threaten Marriages," *The Responsible Community* (Summer 1997), p. 33.

59 Browning et al. (2000), p. 358.

60 John Wall, Thomas Needham, Don S. Browning, and Susan James, "The Ethics of Relationality: The Moral Views of Therapists Engaged in Marital and Family Therapy," *Family Relations* 48:2 (1999), pp. 139–149.

61 Schneider (1996b), p. 205.

62 Browning (1991), pp. 243–277.

63 Habermas (1987), pp. 153–197.

64 Steuerle (in press).

65 Schneider (1996b), p. 195.

66 Nock (1998), pp. 41–42.

67 See the series of articles debating this issue: Paul A. Nabonezny, Robert D. Shull, and Joseph L. Rodgers, "The Effect of No-Fault Divorce Law on the Divorce Rate Across the 50 States and Its Relation to Income, Education, and Religiosity," *Journal of Marriage and Family* 57 (1995), pp. 477–488; Norval Glenn, "Further Discussion of the Effects of No-Fault Divorce on Divorce Rates," *Journal of Marriage and Family* 61:3 (August 1999), pp. 800–802; Joseph Lee Rodgers, Paul A. Nabonezny, and Robert Shull, "Did No-Fault Divorce Legislation Matter? Definitely Yes and Sometimes No," *Journal of Marriage and Family* 61:3 (August 1999), pp. 803–806.

68 For an excellent comparative study of the U.S. and other countries on divorce, documenting the individualistic approach of the American legal system, see Glendon (1989), pp. 188–199.

69 This is a basic tenet of the emerging marriage movement. See Markman, Stanley, and Blumberg (1994).

70 John Gottman, James Coan, Sybil Carrérre, and Catherine Swanson, "Predicting Marital Happiness and Stability from Newlywed Interactions," *Journal of Marriage and Family* 60 (February 1998), p. 14.

71 John Gottman, Sybil Carrérre, Catherine Swanson, and James Coan, "Reply to 'From Basic Research to Interventions,'" *Journal of Marriage and Family* 62:1 (February 2000), p. 272.

72 Scott Stanley, Thomas Bradbury, and Howard Markman, "Structural Flaws in the Bridge from Basic Research on Marriage to Interventions for Couples," *Journal of Marriage and Family* 62:1 (February 2000), pp. 256–264.

73 There are three other options that should be mentioned. There is Building Relationships: Skills for a Life Time prepared by David Olson and based on research of PREPARE/ENRICH from Life Innovations, Inc., P.O. Box 190, Minneapolis, MN 55440. See also Pairs for Peers produced by The Pairs Foundation, LTD., 1056 Creekford Drive, Fort Lauderdale, FL 33326. And finally, see *Partners: A Cur-*

riculum for Preserving Marriages, The American Bar Association Section of Family Law, 750 N. Lake Shore Drive, Chicago, IL 60611.

74 This research program is funded by the NICHD and a group of foundations that includes the Ford Foundation, the Robert Wood Johnson Foundation, the Public Policy Institute of California, the Hogg Foundation, the Fund for New Jersey, St. David's Hospital Foundation, the Commonwealth Fund, and Newark-Beth Israel Healthcare Foundation.

75 Marian Howard and Judith Blamey McCabe, "Helping Teenagers Postpone Sexual Involvement," *Family Planning Perspectives* 22 (January-February 1990), pp. 21–26.

76 Numrich (2000).

77 Robert Bachman and Linda Saltzman, "Violence against Women: Estimates from the Redesigned Survey," *National Crime Victimization Survey Special Report*, U.S. Department of Justice, 1995.

78 For a summary of research on this issue, see the writings of Martin Daly and Margo Wilson (1988) and (1998); also see Waite and Gallagher (2000), p. 151.

79 This information was gathered from a conference held at the University of Chicago Hospitals titled "Bridging the Gap: Adoption and Reproductive Technology," May 5–6, 2000.

80 Habermas (1976), pp. 58, 63–64.

81 Habermas (1990), pp. 201–202.

Bibliography

Amato, Paul. 1998. "More Than Money? Men's Contributions to Their Children's Lives." In Booth and Crouther, 1998.

Amato, Paul, and Alan Booth. 1997. *A Generation at Risk: Growing up in an Era of Family Upheaval.* Cambridge: Harvard University Press.

Bane, Mary Jo, and David Ellwood. 1994. *Welfare Realities: From Rhetoric to Reform.* Cambridge: Harvard University Press.

Becker, Gary. 1991. *Treatise on the Family.* Cambridge: Harvard University Press.

Benjamin, Jessica. 1988. *The Bonds of Love.* New York: Pantheon Books.

Bernstein, Richard. 1983. *Beyond Objectivism and Relativism.* Philadelphia: University of Pennsylvania Press.

Booth, Alan, and Ann C. Crouther, eds. 1998. *Men and Families.* Mahwah, NJ: Lawrence Erlbaum Associates.

Browning, Don. 1987. *Religious Thought and the Modern Psychologies.* Minneapolis: Fortress Press.

———. 1991. *A Fundamental Practical Theology.* Minneapolis: Fortress Press.

Browning, Don, Bonnie Miller-McLemore, Pam Couture, Bernie Lyon, Robert Franklin. 2000. *From Culture Wars to Common*

Ground: Religion and the American Family Debate. Louisville: Westminster/John Knox.

Brundage, James. 1987. *Law, Sex, and Christian Society in Medieval Europe.* Chicago: University of Chicago Press.

Chodorow, Nancy. 1989. *Feminism and Psychoanalytic Theory.* New Haven: Yale University Press.

Daly, Martin, and Margo Wilson. 1988. *Homicide.* New York: Aldine de Gruyter.

————. 1998. *The Truth about Cinderella: A Darwinian View of Parental Love.* London: Heidenfeld and Nicolson.

Dawkins, Richard. 1976. *The Selfish Gene.* Oxford: Oxford University Press.

Derrida, Jacques. 1973. *Speech and Phenomena.* Evanston, IL: Northwestern University Press.

De Waal, Frans. 1996. *Good Natured: The Origins for Right and Wrong in Humans and Other Animals.* Cambridge: Harvard University Press.

Dizard, Jan, and Howard Gadlin. 1990. *The Minimal Family.* Amherst: University of Massachusetts Press.

Dobson, James, and Gary Bauer. 1990. *Children at Risk.* Dallas: Word Publishing.

Doherty, William. 1995. *Soul Searching: Why Psychotherapy Must Promote Moral Responsibility.* New York: Basic Books.

Engels, Frederick. 1972. *The Origin of the Family, Private Property, and the State.* New York: International Publishers.

Etzioni, Amitai. 1988. *The Moral Dimension: Toward a New Economics.* New York: The Free Press.

Furstenberg, Frank, and Andrew Cherlin. 1992. *Divided Families.* Cambridge: Harvard University Press.

Gadamer, Hans-Georg. 1982. *Truth and Method.* New York: Crossroad.

Glendon, Mary Ann. 1989. *The Transformation of Family Law: State, Law, and Family in the United States and Western Europe.* Chicago: University of Chicago Press.

Glenn, Norval. 1997. "Closed Hearts, Closed Minds: The Textbook Story of Marriage." New York: Institute for American Values.

Goode, William. 1993. *World Changes in Divorce Practices.* New Haven: Yale University Press.

Habermas, Jürgen. 1976. *Communication and the Evolution of Society.* Boston: Beacon Press.

————. 1977. *Theory of Communicative Action.* Boston: Beacon Press.

———. 1987. *The Theory of Communicative Action II*. Boston: Beacon Press.

———. 1990. *Moral Consciousness and Communicative Action*. Cambridge: MIT Press.

Hendrix, Harville. 1988. *Getting the Love You Want*. New York: Henry Holt.

Herlihy, David. 1985. *Medieval Households*. Cambridge: Harvard University Press.

Kamper, Charlene. 1996. *Connections*. Berkeley: The Dibble Fund for Marital Enrichment.

Kass, Amy, and Leon Kass. 2000. *Wing to Wing, Oar to Oar*. Notre Dame: University of Notre Dame Press.

Lakoff, George, and Mark Johnson. 1980. *Metaphors We Live By*. Chicago: University of Chicago Press.

Laumann, Edward, John Gagnon, Robert Michael, and Stuart Michaels. 1994. *The Social Organization of Sexuality*. Chicago: University of Chicago Press.

Mack, Dana. 2000. "The Art of Loving: The Science of Teaching Marriage Skills in a Divorce Culture." New York: Institute for American Values.

Marcuse, Herbert. 1955. *Eros and Civilization: A Philosophical Inquiry into Freud*. Boston: Beacon Press.

Markman, Howard, Scott Stanley, and S. I. Blumberg. 1994. *Fighting for Your Marriage: Positive Steps for Loving and Lasting Relationship*. San Francisco: Jossey-Bass.

McLanahan, Sara, and Gary Sandefur. 1994. *Growing up with a Single Parent*. Cambridge: Harvard University Press.

McManus, Michael. 1993. *Marriage Savers*. Grand Rapids: Zondervan Publishing House.

Moore, G. E. 1965. *Ethics*. New York: Oxford University Press.

Niebuhr, Reinhold. 1941. *The Nature and Destiny of Man*. New York: Charles Scribner's Sons.

Nock, Steven. 1998. *Marriage in Men's Lives*. Oxford: Oxford University Press.

Numrich, Paul D. 2000. *The Varieties of Religious Perspectives: What Religions Say about Sexuality*. Chicago: The Park Ridge Center.

Okin, Susan Moller. 1989. *Justice, Gender, and the Family*. New York: Basic Books.

———. 1999. *Is Multiculturalism Bad for Women?* Princeton: Princeton University Press.

Ozment, Steven. 1983. *When Fathers Ruled*. Cambridge: Harvard University Press.

Parrinder, Geoffrey. 1996. *Sexual Morality in the World's Religions.* Oxford: Oneworld Publications.

Paterson, Orlando. 1998. *Rituals of Blood.* Washington, D.C.: Civitas Counterpoint.

Popenoe, David. 1988. *Disturbing the Nest: Family Change and Decline in Modern Societies.* Hawthorne, NY: Aldine de Gruyter.

———. 1996. *Life without Father.* New York: The Free Press.

Popenoe, David, Jean Bethke Elshtain, and David Blankenhorn, eds. 1996. *Promises to Keep: Decline and Renewal of Marriage in America.* Lanham: Rowman and Littlefield.

Popenoe, David, and Barbara Dafoe Whitehead. 1999. "Should We Live Together? What Young Adults Need to Know about Cohabitation before Marriage." New Brunswick: The National Marriage Project, Rutgers University.

Posner, Richard. 1992. *Sex and Reason.* Cambridge: Harvard University Press.

Reed, Ralph. 1994. *Politically Incorrect.* Dallas: Word Publishing.

———. 1996. *Active Faith.* New York: The Free Press.

Ricouer, Paul. 1974. *The Conflict of Interpretations.* Evanston, IL: Northwestern University Press.

———. 1981. *Hermeneutics and the Human Sciences.* Cambridge: Cambridge University.

Rodriguez, Gloria. 1999. *Raising Nuestros Ninos: Bringing up Latin Children in a Bicultural World.* New York: Fireside, Simon & Schuster.

Rorty, Richard. 1979. *Philosophy and the Mirror of Nature.* Princeton: Princeton University Press.

Ryan, Mary. 1981. *Cradle of the Middle Class: The Family in Oneida County, New York, 1790–1865.* Cambridge: Cambridge University Press.

Schneider, Carl. 1996a. "Law and the Deinstitutionalization of the Family." In Popenoe et al., 1996.

———. 1996b. "The Law and the Stability of Marriage." In Popenoe et al., 1996.

Shorter, Edward. 1975. *The Making of the Modern Family.* New York: Basic Books.

Smith, Tom. 1999. "The Emerging 21st Century American Family." Chicago: National Opinion Research Center.

Snarey, John. 1993. *How Fathers Care for the Next Generation: A Four-Decade Study.* Cambridge: Harvard University Press.

Stanley, Scott, Daniel Trathen, Savanna McCain, and Milt Bryan.

1998. *A Lasting Promise: A Christian Guide to Fighting for Your Marriage.* San Francisco: Jossey-Bass.

Steuerle, Eugene. In press. "A Comprehensive Approach to Removing Marriage Penalties." In Whyte, in press.

Stone, Lawrence. 1990. *Road to Divorce: England 1530–1987.* Oxford: Oxford University Press.

Trible, Phyllis. 1978. *God and the Rhetoric of Sexuality.* Philadelphia: Fortress Press.

Vitz, Paul. 1998. "The Course of True Love: Marriage in High School Textbooks." New York: Institute for American Values.

Waite, Linda, and Maggie Gallagher. 2000. *The Case for Marriage.* New York: Doubleday.

Wallerstein, Judith, and Sandra Blakeslee. 1989. *Second Chances: Men, Women, and Children a Decade after Divorce.* New York: Ticknor and Fields.

Weber, Max. 1958. *The Protestant Ethic and the Spirit of Capitalism.* New York: Charles Scribner's Sons.

Weitzman, Lenore. 1985. *The Divorce Revolution.* London: Free Press.

Whyte, Martin, ed. In press. *Strengthening American Marriages: A Communitarian Perspective.* Lanham: Rowman and Littlefield.

Wilson, William Julius. 1987. *The Truly Disadvantaged.* Chicago: University of Chicago Press.

———. 1996. *When Work Disappears: The New World of the Urban Poor.* New York: Knopf.

Winch, Peter. 1958. *The Idea of a Social Science and Its Relation to Philosophy.* London: Routledge and Kegan Paul.

Witte, John. 1997. *From Sacrament to Contract: Marriage, Religion, and Law in the Western Tradition.* Louisville: Westminster/John Knox.

Wolfe, Alan. 1989. *Whose Keeper?* Berkeley: University of California Press.

Final Report
of the
Ninety-Seventh
American Assembly

At the close of their discussions, the participants in the Ninety-Seventh American Assembly on "Reweaving the Social Tapestry: Public Policies for American Families" in Kansas City, Missouri, September 21–24, 2000, reviewed as a group the following statement. This statement represents general agreement; however, no one was asked to sign it, nor did everyone agree with all of it.

Preamble

Fifty-three diverse and experienced professionals from throughout the United States met in Kansas City to bring new light to old and deeply divisive debates about the family. Many participants remember the numerous, often unproductive, debates and struggles to define family policies over the past several decades. Now at the beginning of a new millennium, this group, holding strong ideological differences, was able to find substantial common ground regarding family issues.

In spite of a wide range of problems facing families and

some predictions that they are less important for modern society, we affirm their continuing vital role for the present and future social fabric. Therefore, we hold that public policy should give careful attention to the needs of families. To do this requires a complex weaving together of innovative responses from business and labor, government, the educational system at all levels, civil society, faith based organizations, community based organizations, and the media.

We believe that families are crucial sources for several important individual and social goods:

1. the well-being and development of children;
2. the health and well-being of adults;
3. the vitality and quality of our communities;
4. the preservation of our civil society, nation, and democracy.

Although families can never perform these functions alone, there are no general substitutes for families in accomplishing these tasks.

We acknowledge that the social tapestry supporting families has been weakened due to the considerable pressure and stress of the speed of social change, increasing mobility, the demands of paid work and other economic dynamics, the continuing racial divide, changing cultural norms, the breakdown of the extended family, the unintentional consequences of some government policies, and the growing income disparity that prevents some parents from providing their families with basic needs. These forces have been accompanied by more fatherless families, fueled in the past by rising rates of divorce but most recently by the fact that increasing numbers of children are born out-of-wedlock. Half of such childbearing begins during the teenage years.

Our society is divided on how to respond to these forces. Some people in the United States wish to defend and restore the family patterns of the late nineteenth and the early twentieth centuries that were built around the specialized spheres of wage economy and domestic work. Other people believe that growing family disruption and early out-of-wedlock childbearing are inevitable and that the only solution is increased resources and supports from government. A third response holds that we need significant changes at work and in societal supports to allow individuals to devote themselves to their families as most desire to do. We also need a new cultural strengthening and reformation of both families and marriage—one that is largely, but not exclusively, stimulated by civil society; local communities; and diverse cultural, religious, ethnic, and linguistic traditions. This cultural task would go hand-in-hand with vital new supports from government, law, education, business, labor, and communities.

The spirit and recommendations in this report flow from this third point of view, i.e., the concern to interweave cultural renewal for families with various social and economic supports. It is our hope that this report will help open a new era of fruitful discussion and action on family policy for our country.

This report is divided into three sections—culture, time, and support services for families. Each section describes the problem, identifies the underlying values, and concludes with strategies and recommendations.

Culture: How It Weakens and Strengthens Families

For most Americans, the family is the central institution in their lives: it is the locus of unconditional love and acceptance, the arena where virtues of both independence and obligation to others are cultivated. Although this Assembly does not minimize the strides that the culture has taken in the last few decades—increased status and opportunities for women, greater acceptance of family diversity, and greater cultural support for male engagement in family life—recent cultural developments have placed many American families in jeopardy. In particular, we are concerned that children have suffered from the structural, cultural, and economic devaluation of care giving and commitment in family relationships, the coarsening of our popular culture, and excessive individualism. Parents and would-be parents are encouraged to take their responsibilities to each other too lightly and to underestimate both the challenges and joys of child rearing. Much of our popular culture offers a continuous diet of entertainment that is characterized by an undue focus on sexuality and violence, negative portrayals of marriage and family life, and a distorted picture of romantic relationships.

In the view of this Assembly, our society—especially our public and economic institutions—does not give sufficient time, status, and financial support for the essential task of care giving in families, schools, or childcare centers. We also think that for many people family life has been corroded by an ethos that exalts personal gratification and consumerism over commitment to family relationships. There has been a steady decline in the cultural environment in ways that pose serious threats to children and families. Among other things, these cultural trends have contributed to dramatic increases in family stress, divorce, domestic and child abuse, and child poverty.

Values

This Assembly recognizes and affirms the importance of respecting all persons within a variety of family types. We believe that no family form should be stigmatized. Due to the tremendous cultural, religious, and ethnic pluralism of our nation, public policy must not discriminate against persons based on their family identity, and such policy should be structured in such a way as to "do no harm" to children and families. For the same reason, civil society is the best arena to promote the virtues and values that sustain families. In addition, government ought to respect the cultural diversity and variety of civic institutions.

This Assembly affirms a qualified endorsement of marriage as the ideal family form for the rearing of children. Our endorsement is qualified in four ways:

- First, we specifically endorse an "equal regard" marriage that accords equal dignity, opportunities, and responsibilities for individuals as they pursue their vocations in the family and the public sphere.
- Second, we understand that divorce is a necessary solution in some situations, but we believe that parents of children should work to save a marriage when possible for the sake of the children and the adults.
- Third, we condemn all forms of abuse in marriage.
- Fourth, we do not sanction the social or cultural stigmatization of single-parent families, particularly those that are poor and female headed.

We affirm marriage in part because the last decade has witnessed a surge in social science research indicating that children—on average—do best socially, emotionally, intellectually, and developmentally in a healthy, intact two-parent family. For the purpose of this Assembly, marriage is defined, ideally, as a committed lifelong relationship between two individuals that requires substantive preparation, forethought, and emotional support. There is good news about marriage: recent research indicates that married couples are healthier, wealthier, and live longer.

This Assembly, as with the rest of society, could not find one mind regarding marriage of gay and lesbian couples. Yet, for the common good, we agree that children of such couples must not bear the burdens of our societal debate. Our advocacy, protection, and respect for these and all other children must proceed unhindered by our disagreements. We recommend continued rigorous historical, philosophical, religious, and social science inquiry into this issue.

Our common concern for the stability and well-being of the family leads us to question the punitive and harmful character of public policies that impinge upon families. In particular, we think that federal, state, and local governments need to do more to promote prevention and rehabilitation, particularly with respect to drug policy, juvenile crime, teenage pregnancy, and the foster-care system.

Strategies and Recommendations

Mass media. Much of our popular culture is increasingly toxic for America's families. Accordingly, we recommend that:

• Public leaders exercise their moral authority by challenging the negative products purveyed by our producers of popular culture and by encouraging and rewarding positive portrayals of family life.
• Parents and civic leaders form advisory councils that work with media executives to create family-friendly programing.
• Civil society, not government, take the lead in sanctioning harmful programing with boycotts and public condemnation.
• Effective media and advertising campaigns affirm the importance of marriage commitment and investments of time in family relationships. These announcements should also incorporate the latest social science on relationship skills that promote happy, equal, and committed relationships—including marriage—and publicize the consequences of family dissolution for children.

Government and Civil Society. We think government, and especially civil society, needs to play an important role in promoting healthy families. Accordingly, we recommend the following:

• The government needs to collect and disseminate detailed information on basic demographic trends, on programs that succeed in fostering better relationships, and on social and cultural factors that affect family stability.
• Schools, community based organizations, and religious institutions need to provide opportunities for young people to learn interpersonal skills, as well as the latest research on the value and benefits of marriage and family life. Curricula should promote successful relationship and parenting skills. We also believe that sex education in schools should be a part of broader programs emphasiz-

ing relationship skills and ethics. However, school based programs should provide ways for parents who object to the content of these programs to have their children opt out or not participate.

- Religious institutions need to emphasize their theological and cultural messages about family life in ways that help families deal with the stresses of contemporary society. They should speak out on key matters like family-work issues, poverty, the importance of strengthening faltering marriages, and the effects of divorce.
- Professionals—including but not limited to clergy, therapists, counselors, doctors, lawyers, educators, and youth workers—are encouraged to deepen their knowledge of the recent research on family life, to incorporate this research into their thinking and discourse about family life, and to pass this information on to their constituents.

Individuals. The responsibility for the improvement of American family life does not lie solely with governmental, economic, and civic institutions. Individuals must also play a role in improving American family life. Specifically, we encourage individuals to be more responsible in the following three ways:

- Relationship partners, female and male, should work equally to strengthen their marriages and relationships.
- Parents need to take responsibility for monitoring the kinds of popular culture their children consume and talk to their children early and often about love, responsible sex, and relationships.
- Each individual should accept the discipline of responsibility to family over his or her personal gratification.

Out of Time and Stressed Out: The Time Deficit for American Families

Most Americans love their children deeply and long to spend more time with them. At the same time, most Americans are struggling with an enormous time deficit, which threatens their ability to sustain a healthy, nurturing family life. As a result, many parents are not investing sufficient time in their children's lives; consequently, family relationships and well-being suffer. This over-extension creates stress, which filters into primary relationships with spouses and children. When parents are overextended, relationships with their children often become the most expendable.

Pressure often arises from parents' financial responsibility to provide for their families. This affects families in all income categories. For many poor and middle-class working parents, these stresses result from things such as mandatory overtime or taking multiple jobs to make ends meet. Many affluent parents who pursue career advancement do so at the expense of time with children and family. Children from these homes are often over-programed and suffer stress from excessive parental pressure to achieve.

Many families, however, seem to be adversely affected by a highly materialistic society, fueled by a consumption ethic that infringes on family time, driving both low- and high-income family members to work more hours to fulfill the desire to buy things.

Other consequences include the following:

- Unsupervised children of all ages;
- Marriage/relationship conflict when lack of time creates enormous stress in families;
- Little time for couples to nurture their relationships and meet each other's emotional and interpersonal needs;
- Less bonding time with small children, whose relationships become fragile and tenuous due to a lack of permanence;
- Children are deprived of the unhurried joys and experiences of childhood;
- Though some corporations have made commendable progress, the overall corporate culture is still largely resistant to the level of flexibility necessary to create more time for families to meet the health and emotional needs of children, elders, and other family members.

Ultimately, the time deficit deprives family members of opportunities to interact with community and deprives communities of the talent, creativity, and leadership this interaction can bring.

As a society, we are nearing the point of physical, emotional, and spiritual exhaustion. This Assembly believes that in a competitive, dynamic society making more time available for families will require a major reordering of priorities.

Values

While many Americans value spending time with their family, this desire conflicts with many other ways individual family members want to spend their leisure time such as exploring the Internet, being entertained by the media, shopping, and extracurricular sports. The pursuit of these activities can often pull families in separate directions rather than bring them together.

For many people, home is losing its position as a refuge and place of security and rest. Relationships would strengthen if our lives were simply less harried and if we viewed a lessening of activity as positive and essential for the health of families.

Passing on family culture and tradition requires time and energy that are sorely lacking. In spite of advanced technology that purports to bring people closer together, there is a great hunger for relationships and a yearning for reconnecting.

Deserving of special consideration in our search for increased time and parental involvement are our youngest Americans. Research has shown repeatedly that children require more interaction and nurture from their mothers and fathers than they are presently receiving. Adolescents and young adults also need this attention and support from steady and stable parents, although generally less intrusively.

Strategies and Recommendations

Creating more time for families must be placed near the top of America's public agenda. This will require commitments from the major institutions that affect the family, including the civic, religious, governmental, philanthropic, and corporate communities. These sectors need to increase collaboration to spread important messages to families. They can do this by establishing employment regulations and creating policies and practices that allow more time for parenting.

This Assembly also strongly encourages the following:

- Creating a coordinated, persuasive social-marketing campaign aimed at prioritizing family time and encouraging businesses and parents to take responsibility to make more time for families;
- Calling upon the government and business community to take a closer look at the economic benefits of increasing flexible work policies that would give people more time for their families and community involvement. Primarily, this should include exploring offering sixty-hour workweeks for couples (a combined total of no more than sixty hours worked each week per couple) and reducing workweeks for single parents;
- Advocating changes in treatment of part-time workers by employers, insurance companies, and regulators to allow pro-rated benefits for part-time workers in order to both end worker abuse and allow parents to spend more time with families;
- Investing in public transportation that would serve corporate and family interests by reducing the time workers spend commuting;
- Ending the practice of mandatory overtime;
- Implementing paid parental and family care leave and expanding access to the Family and Medical Leave Act (FMLA) for workers;
- Continuing research into the costs and benefits, especially to the business sector, of time-reducing strategies

for parents in the wage economy. This would be done as a realistic step toward creating proper incentives to keep business and labor moving in a positive direction on family-friendly policies;

• Expanding flexible hours and leave policies for the specific purpose of encouraging parental involvement in the community-based organizations in which their children are involved;

• Reviewing school hours and vacations to make them more congruent with family employment schedules and vacations.

First Do no Harm, Then Lend a Hand: Social Supports for Families

There is strong evidence that families can and do succeed in carrying out their important responsibilities when they are able to acquire the supplementary services they need. The diversity of these services is wide ranging as are their sources, costs, and origins. Each service is a complex, multifaceted, and highly important element affecting the current national debate regarding families. These considerations were an intense focus of this Assembly.

Families today live in an intricate and dynamic society with enormous pressures and equally high expectations. Nearly all families—rich and poor—need to rely, from time to time, on support that comes from outside the family. Such help can have many points of origin and can address many family functions. Existing supports, unfortunately, have fallen short of helping families and sometimes even compound their difficulties. Some problems related to support services include:

• Overall lack of available, affordable services (e.g., child care, elder care, health care, job training, transportation, adequate housing, security, etc.);

• Fragmentation, overlap, and confusion of services as well

as their lack of availability and cumbersome eligibility requirements;
- Inadequate delivery mechanisms at the local level;
- An insensitivity to culture, language, and traditions, particularly for Native American and immigrant non–English speaking families;
- Government sponsored programs that have a corrosive effect on families (e.g., presence of the father in the household disqualifies families from some forms of public assistance, immigration laws that separate family members and deny them needed services, etc.).

Values

Deeply held values must inform the provision of services to families. Foremost among these values is an unequivocal commitment to respect the integrity of the family unit and recognition of the family's strengths. Such respect must be extended to diverse structural, cultural, and religious expressions of family. Without such respect, support services often do more harm than good.

This Assembly reflected upon other values that must inform family support services. Among those reflections are the following:

- Support services must be designed and implemented to undergird the stability, well-being, and permanence of families.
- Families must be supported in a comprehensive, culturally sensitive, and community based manner.
- A coordinated and integrated approach to multifaceted family support services must be developed and maintained. Families cannot be expected to serve as case managers for fragmented systems.
- Faith based organizations, community based organizations, and religious leaders have a unique role to play in encouraging the formulation and delivery of family education and counseling.

• The vast majority of marriages are performed under religious auspices. Religious teachings shape, to a large degree, the ways in which many view the family. Houses of worship have a particular obligation to do a better job of preparing couples for a lifelong commitment to marriage and the family, enriching existing marriages, and saving troubled ones.

Strategies and Recommendations

Innumerable strategies to help families address their needs can be envisioned. However, we believe that some services have more profound and enduring positive outcomes for strengthening and supporting families. As priority social supports, we urge the nation's immediate and focused attention on:

• Accessible and quality health care, a support instrumental to the maintenance of families that requires the consistent and cooperative efforts of business, media, government, schools, and community organizations. The delivery and character of health care services must respect the cultural and religious diversity of families;
• Availability and affordability of high-quality early care and education for all children from birth to age five and after-school programs for children during their school years;
• Governmental policy at all levels must be thoroughly scrutinized to remove penalties and obstacles that confound family functioning, including 1) the elimination of the marriage penalty in both the tax code and in our welfare policy [Temporary Assistance to Needy Families (TANF)] and 2) the destructive practice of requiring poor non-resident fathers to provide child support payments before being allowed to become involved as parents with their offspring;
• Increasing the child tax credit to at least $1,000, raising the ceiling for and phasing out the termination point for the Earned Income Tax Credit (EITC), and increasing

the minimum wage and the dependent care deduction in a timely manner;

- Set as an ultimate goal the elimination of child poverty;
- Establishment of family resource centers and other service delivery mechanisms (e.g., schools, places of worship, housing projects, after-school programs, etc.) that support families with community-defined needs and provide neighborhood connections. The services or programs to be provided may include, but are not limited to pre- and post-marriage education; family, marriage, and relationship counseling; parenting classes; family-life education; health and mental health services; employment counseling and training; youth development; adult literacy and education programs; legal-assistance; childcare; mentoring; education; and mediation services before and after divorce, among others. In divorce mediation, the interests of children should be paramount.

Families will not derive the full benefit of comprehensive support services until and unless a far stronger move toward an integration of services takes place. Many public and private agencies will have to amend their practices and relax age-old tensions and turf wars if families are to reap the benefit of the services offered. Both public and private agencies must become accountable, not only for the provision of quality services, but for professionalism in coordinating such services with other agencies. Only by such practices of accountability can true results be measured, providing evidence that families have indeed been strengthened.

Conclusion

While we cannot and should not turn back the clock, we should respect and look to our traditions for those values that have sustained America's hopes and dreams for more than 200 years. We call upon government, business, and civil society—as well as individuals—to do more to foster family health and stability. We affirm that at the heart of the American dream is a hope for all our children, that each may live in freedom and security to build a good life. This Assembly affirms that, wherever we place ourselves on the ideological spectrum, we can weave a new social tapestry for stronger families and a more united America.

Participants
The Ninety-Seventh American Assembly

▼ **Yolie Flores Aguilar**
Executive Director
Los Angeles County Children's Planning Council
Los Angeles, CA

Azizah al-Hibri
Fellow
National Humanities Center
Research Triangle Park, NC

Sharifa Alkhateeb
President
Muslim Education Council, and the North American Council for Muslim Women
Great Falls, VA

Karen Bartz
Vice President
Hallmark Corporate Foundation
Kansas City, MO

Douglas J. Besharov
Resident Scholar
American Enterprise Institute
Washington, DC

Ann Bookman
Visiting Scholar
Institute for Work and Employment Research
MIT Sloan School of Management
Cambridge, MA

Ellen Bravo
Co-Director
9to5
National Association of Working Women
Milwaukee, WI

◆ **Don Browning**
Alexander Campbell Professor of Ethics & Social Science
University of Chicago Divinity School
Chicago, IL

Zahid Bukhari
Director of Project MAPS: Muslims in American Public Square
Georgetown University
Washington, DC

■ **Blandina Cardenas**
Director/Associate
　Professor
Hispanic Research Center
University of Texas at San
　Antonio
San Antonio, TX

Kathleen E. Christensen
Program Director
Working Families Program
Alfred P. Sloan Foundation
New York, NY

William H. Clark
President and CEO
The Urban League of
　Greater Kansas City
Kansas City, MO

David H. Crary
National Writer
The Associated Press
New York, NY

Bradley Currey, Jr.
Chairman, Retired
Rock-Tenn Company
Atlanta, GA

**The Reverend Thomas
　Davis**
Chair, Clergy Advisory Board
Planned Parenthood
　Federation of America
New York, NY

♥● **Don E. Eberly**
Chairman of the Board of
　Directors/President
The Civil Society Project
National Fatherhood
　Initiative
Gaithersburg, MD

Amy Eddings
News Reporter
WNYC Radio
New York, NY

Barb Friedmann
Executive Director
Coalition for Community
　Collaboration
Overland Park, KS

+ **William A. Galston**
Professor
School of Public Affairs
University of Maryland
College Park, MD

■ **Norval D. Glenn**
Professor of Sociology
College of Liberal Arts
University of Texas
Austin, TX

Peter B. Goldberg
President & CEO
Alliance for Children and
　Families
Milwaukee, WI

Kirk E. Harris
Associate Executive Director
& General Counsel
Family Support America
Chicago, IL

Shamim Ibrahim
President
Niswa Association, Inc.
Lomita, CA

* Rachel L. Jones
CEO
Child Wire, Inc./NPR
Washington, DC

Cherrefe A. Kadri
Attorney
Karamah and Islamic Center
of Greater Toledo
Toledo, OH

* Charlene R. Kamper
Educator
Kamper Curricula
Redlands, CA

Diane Knippers
President
Institute on Religion and
Democracy
Washington, DC

Richard D. Land
President
The Ethics & Religious
Commission
Nashville, TN

▼ Eileen Lindner
Deputy General Secretary
National Council of
Churches
New York, NY

Ted Lobman
President
Stuart Foundation
San Francisco, CA

Deborah Mathis
Fellow
Shorenstein Center
JFK School of Government
Harvard University
Washington, DC

Michael J. McManus
President
Marriage Savers
Potomac, MD

Michele M. Melendez
National Correspondent
Newhouse News Service
Washington, DC

John Monahan
Senior Consultant
Annie E. Casey Foundation
Washington, DC

Donald Ottenhoff
Senior Editor
Christian Century
Chicago, IL

- **Marline Pearson**
Social Science Instructor
Madison Area Technical
  College
Madison, WI

- **Mercedes Perez de Colon**
Vice President of Programs
AVANCE, Inc.
San Antonio, TX

Adam Pertman
Journalist/Author
The Boston Globe
Newton, MA

David Popenoe
Professor of Sociology
The National Marriage
  Project
Rutgers University
Princeton, NJ

Gina Pulliam
Vice President
Community Initiatives
  Division
Heart of America United
  Way
Kansas City, MO

Rip Rapson
President
The McKnight Foundation
Minneapolis, MN

♦ **Gloria G. Rodriguez**
President & CEO
AVANCE, Inc.
San Antonio, TX

Richard Ruiz
Executive Director
El Centro
Kansas City, KS

• **Isabel V. Sawhill**
Senior Fellow
The Brookings Institution
Washington, DC

Marya Schott
Development Director
Youth Opportunities
  Unlimited
Kansas City, KS

Pepper Schwartz
Professor of Sociology
University of Washington
Seattle, WA

- **David A. Smith**
President
Boys & Girls Club of Greater
  Kansas City
Kansas City, MO

Diane Sollee
Founder and Director
Coalition for Marriage,
  Families, and Couples
  Education (CMFCE)
Washington, DC

Ines Talamantez
Associate Professor of
 Religious Studies
University of California at
 Santa Barbara
Santa Barbara, CA

Fasaha M. Traylor
Senior Program Officer
Foundation for Child
 Development
New York, NY

Brad Wigger
Associate Professor of
 Christian Education &
Director, Center for
 Congregations and Family
 Ministries
Louisville Seminary
Louisville, KY

* **W. Bradford Wilcox**
Postdoctoral Fellow
Center for Research on
 Child Wellbeing
Princeton University
Princeton, NJ

Yomi Wronge
Family Writer
San Jose Mercury News
San Jose, CA

Uniting America
Leadership Advisory Group
(In Formation)

Co-Chairs

David R. Gergen	JFK School of Government, Harvard; *The NewsHour* with Jim Lehrer
Karen Elliott House	President, International, Dow Jones & Company, Inc., *Wall Street Journal*
Donald F. McHenry	Georgetown University; Former U.S Ambassador to the UN
Paul H. O'Neill	Chairman, ALCOA

Members

Paul A. Allaire	Chairman, Xerox Corporation
Jonathan Alter	*Newsweek*
Susan V. Berresford	President, The Ford Foundation
Derek Bok	Former President, Harvard University
David L. Boren	President, University of Oklahoma
Michael J. Boskin	Hoover Institution, Stanford University
Bill Bradley	Former U.S. Senator from New Jersey
Joan Brown Campbell	Director of Religion, Chautauqua Institution; former General Secretary, National Council of Churches of Christ
Henry G. Cisneros	Chairman and CEO, CityVista

John F. Cooke	Executive Vice President for External Affairs, The J. Paul Getty Trust
Lee Cullum	Columnist, *Dallas Morning News*
Mario Cuomo	Former Governor of New York
Douglas N. Daft	Chairman & CEO, The Coca-Cola Company
Thomas R. Donahue	AFL-CIO
Peggy Dulany	Chair, The Synergos Institute
Don Eberly	Chair & CEO, National Fatherhood Initiative; Director, Civil Society Project
Marian Wright Edelman	Founder, The Children's Defense Fund
Jeffrey A. Eisenach	President, Progress and Freedom Foundation
Marsha Johnson Evans	Rear Admiral, U.S. Navy (Ret'd); National Executive Director, Girl Scouts of the USA
Dianne Feinstein	U.S. Senator from California
Jim Florio	Former Governor of New Jersey
Robert M. Franklin	President, Interdenominational Theological Center
David P. Gardner	President Emeritus, University of California and University of Utah
John W. Gardner	Graduate School of Business, Stanford University
William George	Chairman & CEO, Medtronic
Peter C. Goldmark, Jr.	CEO, *International Herald Tribune*
Michael Goodwin	President, Office and Professional Employees International Union
William H. Gray III	President and CEO, United Negro College Fund, Inc.
David E. Hayes-Bautista	School of Medicine, UCLA
Bryan J. Hehir, S.J.	Dean, The Divinity School, Harvard University
Antonia Hernandez	President and General Counsel, MALDEF
Irvine O. Hockaday, Jr.	President and CEO, Hallmark Cards, Inc.
Alice S. Huang	California Institute of Technology
Charlayne Hunter-Gault	*The NewsHour* with Jim Lehrer
Frank Keating	Governor of Oklahoma

Robert D. Kennedy	Retired Chairman, Union Carbide Corporation
James T. Laney	President Emeritus, Emory University
Sara Lawrence Lightfoot	Professor of Education, Harvard University
Bruce Llewellyn	Chairman and CEO, Philadelphia Coca-Cola Bottling Co.
Richard G. Lugar	U. S. Senator from Indiana
Lynn Martin	Former U.S. Secretary of Labor; Advisor, Deloitte & Touche LLP; Professor, Northwestern's Kellogg School of Management
David Mathews	President and CEO, Charles F. Kettering Foundation
Elizabeth McCormack	Trustee, John D. and Catherine T. MacArthur Foundation
William J. McDonough	President, Federal Reserve Bank of New York
Dana G. Mead	Former Chairman and CEO, Tenneco Inc.
Yolanda T. Moses	Board Member, The Ford Foundation
Diana Natalicio	President, University of Texas at El Paso
Harry Pachon	President, The Tomas Rivera Policy `Institute
Deval L. Patrick	Vice President and General Counsel, Texaco
Robert D. Putnam	Professor of Political Science, Harvard University
Steven Rattner	Founder, Quadrangle Group LLC
Ralph Reed	Former Executive Director, Christian Coalition
Robert B. Reich	Brandeis University; former Secretary of Labor
William D. Ruckelshaus	Chairman and CEO, Browning Ferris Industries
George Rupp	President, Columbia University
Henry B. Schacht	Chairman and CEO, Lucent Technologies Inc.
Arthur Schlesinger, Jr.	Department of History, City University of New York
Adele Simmons	Vice Chair, Chicago Metropolis 2020

Alan K. Simpson   Former U.S. Senator from Wyoming;
                              Director, Institute of Politics,
                              Kennedy School of Government,
                              Harvard University
Edward Skloot   Executive Director, Surdna Foundation,
                              Inc.
Theodore Sorensen   Partner, Paul, Weiss, Rifkind, Wharton
                              & Garrison
Edson W. Spencer   Former CEO, Honeywell Inc. & former
                              Chair, Ford Foundation
Chang-Lin Tien   Former Chancellor, UC Berkeley;
                              Chairman, The Asia Foundation
Vin Weber   Former Congressman from Minnesota;
                              Partner, Clark & Weinstein
Frank A. Weil   Chairman, Abacus & Associates, Inc.
John C. Whitehead   Former Deputy Secretary of State and
                              Former Chair, AEA Investors Inc.
William Julius Wilson   John F. Kennedy School of
                              Government, Harvard University
Michael Woo   Director of Los Angeles Programs,
                              L.I.S.C.
Daniel Yankelovich   President, Public Agenda Foundation
Alice Young   Chair, Asia Pacific Practice Group,
                              Kaye, Scholer, Fierman, Hays &
                              Handler

About The American Assembly

The American Assembly was established by Dwight D. Eisenhower at Columbia University in 1950. It holds nonpartisan meetings and publishes authoritative books to illuminate issues of United States policy. An affiliate of Columbia, the Assembly is a national, educational institution incorporated in the state of New York. The Assembly seeks to provide information, stimulate discussion, and evoke independent conclusions on matters of vital public interest.

American Assembly Sessions

At least two national programs are initiated each year. Authorities are retained to write background papers presenting essential data and defining the main issues of each subject. A group of men and women representing a broad range of experience, competence, and American leadership meet for several days to discuss the Assembly topic and consider alternatives for national policy.

All Assemblies follow the same procedure. The background papers are sent to participants in advance of the Assembly. The Assembly meets in small groups for four lengthy periods. All groups use the same agenda. At the close of these informal sessions participants adopt in plenary session a final report of findings and recommendations.

Regional, state, and local Assemblies are held following the national session at Arden House. Assemblies have also been held in England, Switzerland, Malaysia, Canada, the Caribbean, South America, Central America, the Philippines, China, and Taiwan. Over 160 institutions have cosponsored one or more Assemblies.

Arden House

The home of The American Assembly and the scene of the national sessions is Arden House, which was given to Columbia University in 1950 by W. Averell Harriman. E. Roland

Harriman joined his brother in contributing toward adaptation of the property for conference purposes. The buildings and surrounding land, known as the Harriman Campus of Columbia University, are fifty miles north of New York City.

Arden House is a distinguished conference center. It is self-supporting and operates throughout the year for use by organizations with educational objectives. The American Assembly is a tenant of this Columbia University facility only during Assembly sessions.

Index